American Dreamer

The Hope and Promise America

Luis B. Pozzolo

American Dreamer

The Hope and Promise America

Copyright © 2022 by Luis B. Pozzolo

All rights reserved.

No part of this book may be reproduced or transmitted in any form or by any means without written permission from the author.

ISBN: 979-8-9853507-1-5

Shared Power Publishing, LLC
PO Box 64236
Tucson, AZ 85728

Printed in U.S.A.

Dedication

- To God – for this second chance and for guiding me to this land.

- To my wife Karen - I have no ability to follow my dreams without her.

- To this land, my new home - and to all of the warriors who keep it alive and safe.

- To my children - who inspire my battles.

- To my father - the warrior - my lighthouse in the tempest.

- To my grandmother - for the hope and the hugs.

- To my uncles Justo and Gustavo - two artists who brought light to my childhood.

Table of Contents

Introduction 5
Chapter 1 The Line 7
Chapter 2 The Newborn 14
Chapter 3 The Unknown 23
Chapter 4 The Door 37
Chapter 5 The List of Shame 43
Chapter 6 The Absence 65
Chapter 7 U-boats in South America 80
Chapter 8 Operation Condor 84
Chapter 9 A New Door 87
Chapter 10 The Black Chief 97
Chapter 11 Democracy Regains a Foothold 107
Chapter 12 The Mujica Factor 111
Chapter 13 Fading 119
Chapter 14 A New Land 127
Chapter 15 The Parallels 139
Chapter 16 The America List 151
Chapter 17 The Ayres Factor 163
Chapter 18 Toxic Connections 178
Chapter 19 Moving Forward 182
Chapter 20 The Border Crisis 186
Chapter 21 Thomas's Flag 202
Chapter 22 Rising to the Challenge 211

Epilogue 220

Introduction

I was born in Uruguay, in the middle of the chaos of domestic terrorism that was sweeping South America. I grew up under a brutal dictatorial military regime. I was able to witness the rebirth of democracy through the passion and political dedication of my Father and his fellow true patriots. He is still my inspiration to this day. The drives within me are inspired by him to settle for nothing less than to live free. I watched in awe as he successfully fought a totalitarian military dictatorship until he was able to see Democracy restored. Then I watched in horror as that Democracy which gave hope to our country was quickly and brutally transformed into the failed promise of Socialism where it remains to this day.

Walk with me as I start my journey on a humid cobbled street in South America. Follow as it leads through a cherry-paneled court room in Kentucky. Continue on with me as I fight the fight my father taught me against the forces of socialism and corruption that ruined my beloved home in Uruguay. I am determined not to let the same thing happen to America, my beloved new home

Travel thousands of miles and dozens of years back with me as I detail the methodical, step-by-step process that moved a free people away from the Inalienable Rights of Self-Governance into a state of government dependency that ruins all economic hopes and dreams. It happened in Uruguay in a matter of just a few decades. It's already happening in America.

As I write this, we are living in times of confusion. We are facing the need for deep reflection and restoration of principles forgotten. I have no illusions - this fight for restoration is not going to be easy. The path to preserve a Republic often grows narrow and difficult at times. History reminds us often that Republics inevitably collapse when their citizen trade their constant vigilance to preserve their precious foundational values for the false security that Socialism or Fascism offers but never delivers.

We will ultimately return to the present so we can stand side by side in this land of the free and the home of the brave. All I ask is that you reconcile how your glimpse into my past should inspire you to fight for our future together while we still have a chance to succeed.

Chapter 1

The Line

October 12, 2003
United States District Courthouse
Lexington, Kentucky

Today, I am number 48 out of 49.

Today - this moment - is the culmination of a 10-year process that was peppered with self-doubt, trials, grief, and revelations. The most difficult part of the entire process was waiting for the arrival of this moment after a decade of uncertainty.

For a goal setter and a planner like me, the days of stress and concern seemed endless at times. The future was veiled in constant uncertainty. The joy and hope that kept me going was mixed with mental 'muggings' that seemed incessant at times. The memories of past realities often refuse to sleep. All of these things make us who we are as we navigate the turmoil between hope and uncertainty.

One of the more recent and troubling memories on this day was the recent death of my beloved maternal grandmother. Even though 5 months had passed, the sadness of things past and my childhood with her still influences the promise of my future.

But this day in particular was different, special. I waited inside the building and stood in the clarity provided by the large windows as I observed the landscape before me. On that beautiful October morning, I replayed those special words that my grandmother taught me, "When one door closes, another opens." I kept that phrase in my mind for decades, insisting that the rule did not apply to me. Until today.

Many of us are like me – pessimistic by nature. Our enthusiasm is drained by lost battles. We often overlook the small victories each new day brings us. This had been my nature for as long as I could remember. At least for this moment today, I was able to defeat the pessimism. Still, it had touched my life more times than I could count. With each visit, it arrived dragging its heavy sack full of memories of the adverse events that had touched my life.

But today a new door truly did open as another slammed closed. In the process, the wisdom of my grandmother was fulfilled. It materialized right in front of my eyes only a short while after her departure from this world. I believe she would have been proud.

This day I stood waiting amidst the bustle of 48 other people. Most of them were speaking different languages. My memories of the closed doors in my past usually led to an open door that was something worse. This time, however, the open door before me led to a new, wide-open world filled with opportunity. The excitement and anticipation kept me playing with the idea that my grandmother was right. In that moment her wisdom touched me deeply.

The formal architecture of the building we were in added to the solemnity of the event. While officials finished their paperwork, I lingered in front of those large windows looking into the world of my future. Flashbacks bombarded me without mercy. So many places and so many times of my life all seemed to come at me without mercy in the same instant. I breathed deeply to stay calm.

I glanced around the paneled room at the 48 strangers assembled here with me today. I wondered where their individual journeys began and how they arrived here. Would this new place require me to carry the same burdens from my past or was this open door somehow different? We had surely navigated different mazes to finish in the same room on this same day. The 49 of us now stood together for the same purpose – to finally complete the process of becoming American citizens. We arrived here in different ways and by different routes. But it was not an accident that we arrived here together to take the final steps of this amazing journey.

In the midst of this gathering, one individual drew me in without uttering a word. I felt as if I could see myself in his eyes - this old man with a full head of thick grey hair. His weathered face was one that had seen more than its share of tragedy. Yet his blue eyes sparkled brightly as he stared off into the distance. Perhaps he was remembering another time and place. He remained suspended in his own thoughts, unaware of my prying eyes.

Those blue eyes could not hide his heavy history. I could see the pain while his gaze seemed to be desperately searching a distant horizon over the many lost years in Czechoslovakia under the Nazis. Then the Communists came and things became even worse.

I imagined a vivid personal history. Crushed dreams of childhood were everywhere; an improvised youth, aching hunger, and constant degradation. And this same tragedy repeated over and over, for an entire generation. I saw the burning reality of the depths of cruelty man can achieve when left unchecked to his own nature.

I felt as if I was walking with him on tiptoes around the brick paved sidewalks in a square in Prague. I could almost feel the moisture hanging in the air as we heard the screams of the wrongly convicted. Then came the gunfire followed by the confusion of the now-orphaned barefoot children. The innocents hide and become shadows. I felt death walking by my side.

Right here in front of me, in those eyes, I found the same capacity for fear I imagined he felt in that square in Prague. There was fear in the heart of that child, now alone. He was a young survivor who was left only with the bitterest memories of cruelty and injustice. The misery and hopelessness of the years that followed would transform that child's smile into a grimace of pain. A shattered childhood that was heaped with torment.

Yet directly in front of me today, I also saw that the smile of that child had mysteriously survived, still alive after almost seventy years. It somehow refused to die even after facing unimaginable atrocities.

Today I was able to see through the eyes of that young Czech boy. We passed through each other's lives, if only for an instant. Although I could feel and see the hardship he endured, I could see goodness. I also understood how the hands of that child remained warm and open to friendship even now; even while carrying the scars that mark the transit of time.

As I was shaking that hand, one of the officials instructed us that it was time to begin. We stood in a formal line, silent, awaiting instructions. The officer counted to confirm we were in correct numerical order. We walked through the building, up the stairs and through a series of doors like well-trained students. We finally reached the courtroom. A set of massive double doors was opened from inside and our line of 49 souls passed silently inside.

We were instructed to sit in the front rows where we remained for several tense minutes. Finally, the bailiff announced, "All rise!" The judge entered, and the ceremony began. I took a final deep breath, relieved that the waiting was over. I examined the paper in my hands one last time reviewing the details of the ceremony. Then, in that court room, 49 souls recited The Oath of Allegiance together in one loud voice,

> "I hereby declare, on oath, that I absolutely and entirely renounce and abjure all allegiance and fidelity to any foreign prince, potentate, state, or sovereignty, of whom or which I have heretofore been a subject or citizen;
> ...that I will support and defend the Constitution and laws of the United States of

America against all enemies, foreign and domestic;

...that I will bear true faith and allegiance to the same;

...that I will bear arms on behalf of the United States when required by the law;

...that I will perform noncombatant service in the Armed Forces of the United States when required by the law;

...that I will perform work of national importance under civilian direction when required by the law; and

...that I take this obligation freely, without any mental reservation or purpose of evasion; so help me God."

The Judge formally addressed the room, speaking on the meaning of Freedom and Liberty. He talked about strength through diversity, about the paths we all walked to arrive, in that room, on that day. While he was acknowledging our diverse origins and spoke about our childhoods in other lands, the soft cry of a newborn arose from the rear of the courtroom. It seemed a bit out of place but it instantly transported me back in time, to another brick-paved street decades before.

Chapter 2

The Newborn

It was almost midnight on August 25, 1971, winter season in Uruguay. The cobblestone streets were wet from the steady torrent. A few street lights remained, hanging by some miracle. The wind refused to be still, scattering the light everywhere and nowhere while the Independence Day celebration was still going strong.

Out of that cold winter night, an influential political figure stepped into the Spanish-style building with high double doors and windows. It was a historic building that had been transformed into a private hospital. The man had come, tired and wet from a long day of ceremony and speeches on Independence Day. He is quietly directed to one particular room. Once inside he asks everyone to kindly leave. As the door is closing behind them, he pulls up a heavy wooden chair to sit close to the cradle in peace and solitude. Outside the wind and rain continues to rage.

He watches as the newborn experiments with the new world of vivid colors, sounds, sensations, and challenges. This veteran of life, this imposing leader, arrived with plans to give his first talk to the newborn. Perhaps he planned to convey the wisdom gathered over a lifetime while sharing the condition of the world. Perhaps he would share his hopes for the future as would any parent.

The talk between the world-wise father and his new son perhaps included grim description of political stability now at risk. Perhaps it was about a new scourge facing his beloved country that emerged only a decade ago. Perhaps he shared his concern of how to resolve the new challenges faced by the ill-equipped leaders in the unprepared democratic political system.

One thing was certain. Tonight, the man was trying to reconcile how the promise of this new democracy would improve the uncertainty of the child's future. For this new father, the future of his nation was somehow tied directly to the future of his newborn son.

* * * *

In 1971, the nation of Uruguay was on rocky ground. Back in the 1960's it was unique among South American countries for its affluence and sociopolitical stability.

Economic prosperity had fostered the growth of a large middle class and a stable government that allowed a wider degree of democratic and civil freedoms than any South American country. Such a peaceful society was maintained a very small army and police force. In 1968, there were only about 12,000 men in the armed forces and fewer than 22,000 police to keep order in a population of approximately 3 million.

Following the Korean War, a slump in international demand had decimated the market for the nation's two principal exports - wool and beef. The downturn brought massive unemployment, inflation, and a steep decline in the standard of living. The population was uneasy about the future and questioning the wisdom of political leadership. The uncertainty and fear opened the door to a push by the Soviet Union that allowed socialism to take root through a revolutionary guerilla movement.

The revolutionary group's official name was Movimento de Liberacion Nacional. They were known among the people simply as the Tupamaros (named for Tupac Amaru, the last member of the Inca royal family who was murdered by the Spanish in 1571).

The movement was founded in 1963, by Raul Sendic, a law student studying in the capitol of Montevideo. Because the country was so urbanized (over 80% lived in large towns or cities), Tupamaros concentrated their anarchist activities almost exclusively in and around the capitol since that was where more than half the population of the country lived. As with most other South American guerrilla groups, they started as a student political organization. Very soon after, they chose to adopt the tactics of armed struggle. They drew their initial membership from mostly young, radical, middle-class students, and white-collar workers. They organized as independent cells. For security reasons the groups were limited to only four or five members. The group leader was the only link to the other cells. Security was tight and the practice no one was told any more than he or she needed to know for any particular operation.

From 1963 to early 1968, the Tupamaros concentrated on funding their warfare mostly by robbing government run banks, gun shops, and private businesses. These activities supplied much-needed capital for financing the terrorist activities designed to undermine legitimate government.

The Tupamaros goal was to make the government look powerless to maintain peace and security. They chose targets that would invite a level of retaliation that would make the government look heavy-handed in response to Tupamaros activities. Tactics included political kidnappings, robbery, and harassment of government security forces. The

Tupamaros used the kidnappings as an alternative to assassinations and to further show the impotence of the government.

These actions had a severe psychological impact on the supporters of Democracy. They also served to embarrassed government officials, some of whom had influential friends and diplomatic figures snatched off the street. They were held in so-called "people's prisons" hidden right under the nose of the government deep within Montevideo, the very seat of power.

The growing Marxist indoctrination in high schools and universities provoked a wave of unmet demands followed by rioting among students and labor unrest; a state of national emergency was declared in June 1968 which would last until late 1972. It was during this crisis that the Tupamaros staged their first political kidnapping.

Ulysses Pereyra was the President of the State Telephone Company and he disappeared off the street without a trace. When police began to search the campus of the National University, the students started a riot where one student was killed. The Tupamaros released Pereyra unharmed five days later but the damage had been done. The government had looked helpless and impotent.

More political kidnappings followed to further chip away at the government. In September 1969, Tupamaros kidnapped a leading banker and held him for ten weeks, in support of a strike by employees of his state bank.

The country faced continuing economic crises during most of the 1960s and 1970s. The United States government feared that the leftist Tupamaros would topple the Uruguayan government so they provided with security training and equipment plus other forms of economic aid. The United States also helped enhance the counter-insurgency techniques of the Uruguayan police. In the mid-1960s, those efforts were consolidated within the Uruguay's National Agency of Information and Intelligence run by the police. This agency received guidance from a veteran FBI agent Dan Mitrione. The agent was a naturalized American citizen, born in Italy. He was also ex-CIA.

On July 31, 1970, the Tupamaros insurgents kidnapped Mitrione and demanded the release of one hundred fifty Tupamaro prisoners held by the Uruguayan government. If they failed to release them within 10 days, Mitrione would be executed. A message from the U.S. government to the struggling Uruguayan government on August 9, 1970 made it clear that the U.S. was determined to keep Tupamaros insurgents from killing Mitrione as promised. The U.S. ambassador reported that a threat was made to the insurgent leaders that members of a special tactical teams would take action against them and their relatives if Mitrione were killed.

During the ten days Mitrione was held prisoner, the U.S. government went to great lengths to secure his release. The Nixon administration pressured the Uruguayan government to negotiate, to offer ransom and, in the words of President Richard Nixon himself, "spare no effort to secure the safe return of Mr. Mitrione."

Dan Mitrione's body was found on the morning of August 10, 1970. He had been murdered by the Tupamaros right after their demand for release of the guerilla prisoners was not met. He had been killed on the 11th day.

Documents posted later by the National Security Archive contain evidence that the government of Uruguay unleashed several death squads in the wake of Mitrione's execution. Their goal was to hunt down and kill the insurgents and their families as promised. Documents would later provide proof that these extra-judicial death-squad operations were a policy tool of the Uruguayan and United States government working together.

* * * *

The man sits in the chair, trying to stay awake. The cold night silence claimed the hospital in apparent peace, but the man knows what is coming so he keeps whispering words of comfort to the restless infant.

He remains there throughout most of Independence Day. He watches his newborn son, who is blissfully unaware of his uncertain future. The man knows that the atrocity of terrorism will bring more death and more instability. The death of the American, Dan Mitrione, had had unleashed more violence, more kidnapping, more torture and more death.

It is difficult for the man to understand what the future holds. His is a small country with deep democratic roots, but with leaders who are young, and often both naïve and stubborn. He is a one of the few respected and influential leaders. He was elected Senator of the Colorado Party who had brought stability, economic prosperity, and the eight-hour workday law. His was the party that supported the free expression that was the cornerstone of this fragile democracy. His was the party that discussed the issues face-to-face with everyone, the party that brought a productive plan to make the country successful in the international market.

But for many people this was not enough. The Cold War brought new techniques for the always-prepared conspirators, to demand more. No matter what concessions were made, they would cry, "Not enough!" and bring more violence. The timing for making these unreasonable demands could not have been worse. The country was suffering from the impact of international changes and depreciation of our markets. The Tupamaros not only knew they this, they used it against their own people and country. But socialism only has one end game – control. Thus, the killing, violence, torture, and robbery continued.

It was on that Independence Day in Mercedes, Uruguay in 1971, that I was born in the middle of this chaos.

Chapter 3

The Unknown

In August 1961, Ernesto 'Che' Guevara visited Montevideo and gave a speech recognizing Uruguay's democracy and the existence of freedom and liberty. At that time Che was already a socialist icon. He was clearly the most prominent figure of the Marxist revolution in Latin America. At the time, he called for violence ONLY as a last resource. In a key section of the speech Che said:

> *"Force is the last resource that is left for the people. The people can never renounce force, but force should only be used to fight against the perpetrator who uses force indiscriminately.*
>
> *And to us - it may seem strange that we talk about it, but it is true - we began the path of a armed struggle, very sad path, very painful, I have the personal experience to say that in Latin America, and in each of it countries I have visited, in some form, I can assure you that in "our America", in the current conditions, there is not a country where, as in Uruguay, is allowed diversity of ideas .There*

are different ways of thinking, and it is logical; and I know that the members of the Government of Uruguay are not in agreement with our ideas. However, this Government allows the expression of these ideas here, in the University and in the territory of the country that is under the Uruguayan Government. In such way that is something that has not been achieved, or much less, in other countries of the Americas.

You have something that we need to protect, precisely the right to express ideas; the right of advancing by democratic channels to create someday these conditions in the Americas, so that we can all be brothers, so there is no exploitation of man by man nor follow the exploitation of man by man, without the shedding of blood, without which there will be nothing of what was produced

In Cuba, when the first shot was fired, you never know when will be the last. Because there was not one last shot on the last day of the Revolution; we had to keep shooting. Shot at, we had to be tough, we had to punish with death to some people; if we are attacked again, we have returned to attack once more, and we will continue to attack."

Guevara told the Uruguayan people on that winter day in 1961, that the revolution reserves the right to use violence as a last resort also to bring freedom or escape oppression. Funny how the 'use-of-force' justifications for the revolution just keeps growing. He also told them that since these rights already existed in Uruguay that a revolution may not be needed here. That message never found a home with the Tupamaros.

My personal experience confirms an interesting reality that made the countries of Latin America, "our America", so ripe for socialism. Not a single country other than Uruguay has a tradition that encourages free expression and diversity of ideas. At best, it is barely tolerated but most often any criticism of the government is just not permitted. There may be different ways of thinking throughout Latin America but they are permitted only so long as they agree with the government. By contrast, the government of Uruguay generally allowed the expression of these ideas. In such a way, Uruguay offers something that had not been achieved in any other country of the Americas except Canada and the U.S.

Uruguay has also been described as the Switzerland of South American because of the beauty of the mountains and the forests. Yet unlike Switzerland, Uruguay was ultimately overtaken by the false promises of socialism. Still, one questioned lingered for me since I was a teenager. Why, in the presence of this freedom did people like Che Guevara come to our country to spread the nightmare of terrorism and bloody Marxist revolution.

The United States in those days acknowledged and protected the freedom of speech found in their Bill of Rights. Uruguay needed to do this as well. Uruguay needed to protect the right to express ideas and the right of advancing them by democratic channels if we hoped to someday create these conditions. America was not perfect, but protecting those rights helped create a far better environment for its citizens We long for a place where we can all be brothers and where exploitation of man by man using violence or intimidation is not an everyday experience. This exploitation and the shedding of blood was widespread in Cuba and the tide was rising throughout South America. Che was right about one thing. When the first shot is fired, you do not know whether or not it will be the last or when it will end.

Che Guevara left Uruguay and, several years later, was captured by the CIA-backed Bolivian army. He was executed the next day. He had spent his life promoting Marxist socialism and violent revolution so no surprise that he ended up dying in the whirlwind of violence he helped create. Meanwhile, the group of radical Tupamaros he addressed in Uruguay did not adopt the plan for a socialist revolution of the type Che had proposed. They had a favored plan of their own.

In secret, they assembled a destabilization plan based on terror and anarchy. It would forty years for them to do so but they ultimately succeeded in destroying the democratic system in a way that plunged Uruguay into the darkness of Socialism.

* * * *

Dawn crept through the windows while the man remained at the hospital. Many of those who were present the previous day had returned to their homes. The man decided to remain, sleeping on a sofa in the same room with his son. The past few days were long and exhaustion carried him into a deep sleep. It was still raining outside, softly this time. Around him one could hear the sounds and voices of those returning to work. The life of a small town awakening to the day continued to filter into the hospital room through the tall windows. The man, still exhausted, slept as he dreamed of his own childhood days gone by.

In his dream, he sees the end of a cobblestone alley that dropped to the bank of the river. There sits a humble house with a well-tended garden. A few blocks away he could see the graveyard. Its entrance was shaded by tall palm trees and eucalyptus. The cemetery is bathed in sunlight and the day is very humid. It is surrounded by white walls and unpaved streets. Nearby, neighborhood children gather in the light of day to offer their services to those who come to visit the dead.

Their services include fetching water, cleaning of the tombs, and gathering flowers. In this way, these children could provide some small relief to the hunger and misery in their homes. Life is not easy for these children as they swarm near the cemetery looking for hope and handouts. Their imaginative spirits and the optimism that remains bound in the heart of a child helps them pass each day while hoping for one profitable patron. Perhaps tomorrow will be the day when an important customer arrives buying more flowers, needing an errand, anything.

As the man continues to dream, the rest of the world is at war. The reminders are constant and can frequently be heard on the radio. The latest news and events of this War in Europe are broadcast constantly. The stories would soon lead to D-day and the dismantling of the Nazi war machinery in Europe. The man remembers how he and his childhood friends hung on these stories from the radio. It continually sparked their imagination. Nearby, they improvised wooden rifles and played their own non-deadly war games in the lush vegetation.

Life is not easy in neighborhoods like this. Each day brings new challenges. Each day everyone seeks new ways to survive and make their poverty less painful. Unfortunately, most eventually succumb to the absence of hope. But not all will be trapped in this vicious circle; some will succeed and pursue their dreams beyond their existing meager horizons. Most, however, will remain.

* * * *

The cry of the newborn awakens everyone. The man groans as he is drawn back to the present. He rises and heads off in search of coffee while the nurses perform their duties. Another new day.

The sun has not fully risen. At the top of the nearby hills, the raindrops covering the lush leaves begin to sparkle. Everything begins to take life and move about. In such a land, hope is there in everything that exists. It is renewed by the light and the encouragement of the heaven and earth. The old land is daily overshadowed by each new day, a new hope, another instance.

But August is also mid-winter in Uruguay. It is the fear of the poor as the cold chills through to the bone. The improvised wood stoves of their meager houses are never enough. The nights become endless. The wind blows, never relenting to allow a return to stillness. At times it seems to be a chilling call, like the howl of a beast that pierces through everything with murderous rage. The pitiful bark of a distant dog shakes the quiet, its misery almost seeming to solidify in the freezing air. As the sun rises, the fallow fields and roads reappear - hard with frost and loneliness.

The new day opens the sky with vague clarity. The light of a new day is reflected in the puddles; grasslands gleam as though planted in glass. In the surrounding poverty, all has been gnawed by the misery - the clothes, the joy, health. In many ways it is like a concentration camp with walls made only of the darkness. Is misery not a constant war of its own? If so, we are pawns in a war that we did start but are forced to join. The cold August makes the passage of the days an eternity, without resources, hope dies inside a little each day.

The morning that brought the man back to reality is filled with obligations and responsibilities. With the dawn arrives, the daily ache of a vibrant but sick country that is incubated with a new disease of Socialism. This time the political chaos comes arrives at the hands of the Tupamaros.

The route from the hospital on Columbus Street to the Capital takes about four hours by car. A quick farewell and the journey back to Montevideo begins with the man's few political staffers. The demands are daunting. The actions in the shadows by the Tupamaros has spawned a larger and more deadly monster – the military death squads. They had been created to fight the armed insurrection that the Tupamaros were bringing against the nation. The kidnapping and killing that the Tupamaros launched daily was now being answered with secret squadrons of death. Every time those in absolute power are threatened by violence, they respond in kind and usually to the extreme. What is offered as a cure only brings more death while corrupting men and institutions for years.

The two-way highway to Montevideo is plagued with military checkpoints. Finally, the car arrives at the Capital about noon. The timing is perfect for a fast lunch and a change of suits. The day would finish of endless meetings with different officials. The trip into the city was not easy. The road was crowded with traffic and the city wore new clothes on its walls. Endless slogans, graffiti, and badly-done murals all showed a new chaotic society coming. In addition to the political crisis, the guerrilla movement was worsening the economic crisis as well.

Montevideo is Uruguay's largest city as well as its capitol and main port. It rests on Uruguay's southern coast along the eastern banks of the Rio Santa Lucia. It grew from a settlement established in 1724 by Bruno Mauricio de Zabala. It is the southernmost cosmopolitan capitol city in the Americas and third most southern in the world. It is a vibrant city with a very rich cultural life. It is also the main hub of the nation's commerce and higher education. Uruguay's first university, the Universidad de la República, was founded there in 1849. The architecture of Montevideo reflects its history, ranging from colonial to Art Deco with many Spanish, Portuguese, Italian, and French influences.

Montevideo is also home to Punta Carretas – an imposing four-story prison where each floor contained 48 cells. Built at the beginning of the twentieth century, the prison became famous in 1931 when a group of eight anarchists dug a tunnel and escaped. On this day, however, it housed a few common criminals and over a hundred Tupamaros terrorists on its second and third floors.

A few days after Independence Day in Uruguay in 1971, the government in Montevideo announced to a shocked nation that almost all of the Tupamaros, including their main leaders, had escaped. It was one of the largest escapes of terrorist prisoners in South America. The Tupamaros had organized a decoy attack in neighboring town to distract and draw the security forces away from the real operation. Meanwhile, another group of Tupamaros occupied a house located near the front of the prison. Inside the house was the end of a tunnel that served as the escape hatch. The tunnel from the 1931 anarchist escape was once again used to facilitate that day's escape 40 years later. The prison break came not long after the completion of Operation Abuse, which had been the military's operation that resulted in the imprisonment of these one hundred eleven militants of the Tupamaros movement. September 6, 1971 was a dark day for democracy in Uruguay.

Among the escapees was José Mujica, a Marxist who would later be captured and returned to prison only to escape once again. Mujica would eventually rise to power many years later as Uruguay's socialist president. Also freed in the prison break was Eleuterio Fernandez Huidobro who would one day become Defense Minister of Uruguay.

These terrorists continued to believe that taking a democratic government by force to impose their Marxist model would somehow bring freedom and liberty even though it never had and never would.

My grandfather had been a police Sergeant for more than twenty years. He lived through the sedition of the Tupamaros. Every night he left home to serve, leaving his family alone. On some of those nights he might receive word that one of his fellow officers had been wounded or killed. The uncertainty of fighting an enemy that had no uniform and who hid in the shadows was like a crushing stress in his life.

After the escape from prison, Mujica and the other main Tupamaro leader, Raul Sendic organized new attacks. One of them happened in the city of Mercedes where my grandfather lived and served. One night, while out for his usual rounds through the city, he saw group of men containing Sendic and several others. He walked around the railway station then headed down to the river beside a bridge where he noticed a boat crossing toward him. The boat reached the shore and landed in the dark. From the boat, another Sergeant came ashore and the two of them gave the command for the men to stop and identify themselves. The response came not in words but in lead, as the four or five armed fired on them, only to then vanish into the night.

In those days police did not have radios to call for help. They only had a whistle and a .38 revolver with the bullets that the policeman had to buy himself. The Sergeant returned fire, without luck, but he succeeded in identifying Raul Sendic, as one of the members of the group. He alerted his Captain, who received the information but didn't believe the Sergeant. The very next day an attack was launched against the Captain in the same town. He was hospitalized with several bullet wounds. Several the witnesses identified Raul Sendic as part of the group.

In August 1972, Raul Sendic was again captured after he was confronted by the Navy in Montevideo. Sendic survived a direct shot to his face and was returned to prison after recovering from his wounds.

Public security was a growing concern to the few million souls living under the random attacks by an estimated 5,000 Tupamaros. The streets were not secure even under martial law and law-abiding citizens had their liberties greatly restricted. It was not a good idea to be outside with the Military and Police posting in the streets to look for an invisible enemy, one without a uniform. Mistaken identities were not uncommon.

Uruguay had recently been a society of peace, full of life as it tried to nurture its young democracy. All Democracies are a work in progress as every society has its problems to solve. But how could it be honorable to attempt to take power and to impose another economic regime through violence and crime?

The Tupamaros called themselves heroes, saviors, as if they were saving a society from democracy by using Marxism. The Military and Police were able to slowly defeat them and held many of them in prison for over a decade. Even so, those years in prison did little but delay the Tupamaros from seizing power and ultimately ushering in socialism. Their "romantic" view of armed revolution opened the Pandora's box which brought more crime, more murder, and the destruction of our Republic. And I grew up in the middle of it all.

Chapter 4

The Door

Mercedes, the town of my youth, was a quiet place on the south shore of the Rio Negro. The city is divided into a number of neighborhoods. The homes of the prominent landowners were grouped in a line along one bank of the river; to the south, east and west were the shantytowns, where poverty was visible and widespread.

My early years were spent in a neighborhood somewhere between these two extremes. We lived a few blocks away from the river. Our neighborhood was mostly small modest colonial style homes with internal patios and thriving gardens. The area contained some new buildings and a few of the streets had wide sidewalks covered with tiles. There was little traffic, so playing soccer was a common activity. The days were endless and the nights were devoured by the darkness. What little light there was came from a single public light at each corner.

Life was much simpler in the years before the internet. There was radio and only one TV channel transmitting from 7 p.m. until midnight. The children played in the neighborhoods in search of new ideas, new games, and new ways to make mischief.

These were also the days the country was being shaken by the scourge more destructive than its routine economic or social problems. A new system of Marxist socialism was being forced into people's lives by the hand of the Tupamaros. The Tupamaro movement behind it all brought a wave of lawlessness to the country. It was a perfect storm combining looting, theft, assault, kidnapping, and murder to achieve their political ends. This was an imported movement trained and financed by foreign governments, most especially the USSR. Marxism everywhere starts by planting seeds of doubt and discontent in the hearts and minds of the underclass. Then come the violent actions and demands to simply turn over the reins of power to them despite offering no assurances things will be better with them in control. What madness!

It was now September 9, 1971 - three days after the Tupamaro prison break. Several days later, President Jorge Pacheco Areco drew the armed forces into the fight against the Tupamaros. It was a decision he would soon regret.

New elections followed in November, 1971. A new government was sworn in on March 1, 1972, headed by President Juan Maria Bordaberry. The role of the Armed Forces in the political life continued to grow and it was having an impact.

A year later, February 8, 1973, President Bordaberry realized it was critical that he regain control back from the military. He first replaced the Minister of National Defense, Armando Malet, with retired general Antonio Francese. That same morning, Francese called a meeting with the commanders of all three branches of Uruguay's armed forces. Only the commander of the Navy attended.

The state-run television channel reported that the heads of the Army and the Air Force announced they were "unaware" of the orders of Minister Francese and called instead for the President to surrender his baton and resign. Later that night, a private TV channel broadcast President Bordaberry's announcement that he would keep Francese in the Ministry and would convene a rally at Independence Plaza in support of his government.

Early on February 9, the Navy used barricades to support and facilitate the planned rally at the entrance to the Old City of Montevideo. At the same time, the Army moved tanks on to the streets to stop them and occupied several radio stations from which they called upon the members of the Navy to join their forces in opposition.

The commanders of the Army and Air Force then issued Communicado #4. It was a joint statement that demanded that the government renounce or renegotiate Uruguay's foreign debt, reduce unemployment, promote many social and economic reforms, root out corruption, redistribute land, reorganize public administration, increase exports, and revise the tax laws. Furious attempts were made to negotiate with these newly-rebellious military commanders so that President Bordaberry could retain power.

Meanwhile, key officers in the Navy began refusing the orders of vice-admiral Juan José Zorrilla. Those officers finally announced their full support for the Army and Air Force. Zorrilla then relinquished command of the Navy, leaving all three branches of the military now opposed to the President. This left President Bordaberry with little choice but to accept the stated demands of the military in order to remain in office.

A number of changes were instituted that allowed the military to solidify its grip on power, including the President's decree to dissolve the General Assembly. He did so on June 27. 1973. The President made this statement during a speech he gave the same day he dissolved the Senate and House of Representatives.

> "...*this step that we had to give is not going to limit the freedom or rights of the human person, for this reason we have also committed those functions to the Council of State. On top of all that, the Uruguayan people will never cease to exercise their freedom*".

Disbanding the General Asembly essentially completed the last step necessary to transfer power to the military. The military council tried to maintain an illusion that Uruguay was still being run by civilian government but the citizens were not fooled. The reality was simple - their military coup was now complete.

On the same morning, in response to the coup, the secretary of the CNT (National Convention of Workers) began the longest general strike in the history of the country. It lasted 15 days and crippled commerce. It also sent a message that the military might hold power but they did not hold it all.

My father, an elected Senator, was dismissed from office by the coup forces. The new extremist government immediately started circulating blacklists of not only

Tupamaros and their supporters, but anyone who didn't agree with the military regime. Democracy was now being viewed by the people as a weak system because it had neither survived the onslaught from the socialist Tupamaros nor was it able to withstand an armed power grab from the military.

People like my father who believed in freedom, liberty, democracy, and in our Republic as a political system, were also on these blacklists. Nobody dared to employ or protect those who were named. On a cold winter's evening, the gray front door of our house opened. Outside, dressed in a brilliant gray suit stood my father. Behind him, parked in the street, was a large blue American sedan. I'm still able to close my eyes and feel the chill of that evening. The sights and sounds of it remain vivid in my memory.

It was 1975 and my father was fleeing the country to seek refuge in Paraguay. My mother decided that the she and I would stay back on the other side of the door. That door became like a wall between my father and me that would not crumble for many years. I was only 4 years old that day but I somehow knew that my life was changing forever. I had no way to know that it would be more than a decade until my father would reappear behind yet another door - wearing another gray suit and looking as elegant as the day he departed.

Chapter 5

The List of Shame

Marxist socialism was being widely exported by the Soviet Union and introduced into countries around the world during the 1960s. Many of these "revolutionaries" were trained and financed by foreign governments, primarily the USSR. By this time, the Tupamaros were the dominant socialist movement in Uruguay even while being hunted by the military. They had a commitment to violence in many forms as part of their long tradition. They brought a wave of crime to the country that was unprecedented.

Everything was open season: looting, theft, assault, kidnapping, and murder. My goal in this section is to list every victim and crime I could find that was attributed to them. I present this list to help you understand that I want to preserve a record of the events of those days. We also do not want the victims to be lost in time. We want them to be remembered! History must be reported based on truth and that truth is sometimes not pleasant.

This source for much of this information can be found in local documents such as news articles and public records. Some of it comes from various Wikipedia posts as well. It is well-documented that Wikipedia information is open-sourced and that little or no editorial control is exercised to confirm the accuracy of the postings. To address this fact, the information was widely cross-checked against footnoted documents and to other sources.

Thefts and robberies

1) September 12, 1964: assault on a branch of the Bank of Collections taking US $5,800.

2) May 13, 1966: assault on a branch of the Bank Workers' Housing taking US $4,600.

3) November 22, 1966: assault on a branch of the Banco Popular stealing $7,270.

4) December 14, 1966: assault on a local of FUNSA (main tire company of Uruguay)

5) January 18, 1968: assault on a branch of the Union of Banks of Uruguay appropriating $450.

6) September 10, 1968: attack on the Bank of London and South America stealing $20,000.

7) October 2, 1968: assault to branch of the Bank of Credit taking $700.

8) October 3, 1968: assault on Arroyo Seco branch - Commercial Bank stealing $12,860.

9) October 4, 1968: assault on the branch of Malvin Credit Bank stealing $1,040.

10) October 7, 1968: assault on the Bank of London $47,200 stolen.

11) October 18, 1968: attack on the Society of Banks, stealing $23,560.

12) November 29, 1968: assault on Hotel Casino Carrasco taking $25,000.

13) October 24, 1968: assault on the branch of the Commercial Bank –$13,700.

14) November 1, 1968: assault on the branch" Goes" taking $13,316.

15) December 10, 1968: assault on Mercantile Bank – $1,880.

16) December 12, 1968: assault on Popular Bank appropriating $13,700.

17) December 31, 1968: $48,000.

18) January 7, 1969: stealing $32,000.

19) February 16, 1969: assault on the Financial Monty $2,400.

20) February 18, 1969: assault on Casino San Rafael of Punta del Este, $220,000 stolen.

21) March 13, 1969: assault on Bank "Fray Bentos" taking $60,000.

22) April 11, 1969: Assault on the Bank of Credit, Collections and "Sayago" Society $22,000.

23) April 23, 1969: Branch of the Commercial Bank: $11,000.

24) June 5, 1969: Two banks located in Montevideo and an armored van: $54,000.

25) 16 July, 1969: theft of the flag of the "33 Orientales" (flag used in the Independence war).

25) July 31, 1969: First Bank National City Bank – amount stolen unknown.

26) September 30, 1969: Offices of the National Cash Register – $4,000.

27) October 2, 1969: Mayor of San Jose assaulted while delivering salaries $36,000

28 & 29) October 8, 1969: the call is made "takes of Pando" with raids and attacks to the Bank Sugar Loaf, the B. R. O. U. and the Bank of Pando as well as to the U. T. E. , to the police station and the Fire Brigade headquarters, stealing a sum estimated at between $250,000 and $400,000.

30) October 15, 1969: House of National Currency exchange - $240,000.

31) November 12, 1969: Branch of Montevideo Bank - $6,000.

32) November 25, 1969: Branch of the Popular Bank - $28,000.

33) November 25, 1969: Through the use of fraudulent checks takes $104,000.

34) December 29, 1969: Commercial Bank - security guard Juan Techera Bovadilla, died.

35) January 23, 1970: Bank Branch of Pocitos $1,200.

36) January 24, 1970: Retirement Fund of the staff of the Jockey Club of Montevideo - $ 4,000.

37) February 5, 1970: Assault Firepot - $2,220.

38) February 13, 1970: Assault of leather factory o: $4,000.

39) February 24, 1970: Salto City Branch of the BROU - $80,000.

40) March 9, 1970: Branch of the Union of Banks of the Uruguay - $4,000.

41) March 12, 1970: Palestinian Bank, an aluminum factory, plastics factory - $22,000.

42) March 30, 1970: Branch of the French and Italian bank: Amount stolen unknown.

43) April 5, 1970: Succession MAILHOS dollars and pounds - value of $300,000.

44) April 7, 1970: Offices of "Castro Refrigerator" in Montevideo - $1,050.

45) April 14, 1970: Branch of the Mercantile Bank - $14,000.

46) May 25, 1970: assault on Cinema Square - 1 million pesos.

47) May 30, 1970: Offices of the National Cash Register - $16,000.

48) June 23, 1970: Bank of the Uruguay Palestinian - $72,000.

49) July 1, 1970: Branch of the Bank of London and South America - $56,000.

50) July 17, 1970: Branch of the Society Model of Banks of Uruguay - $2,800.

51) July 20, 1970: Signature OTTONELLO Brothers - $7,200.

52) July 22, 1970: Branch of the Society of Banks of the Uruguay - $8,000.

53) July 31, 1970: Offices of the Textile CUOPAR - $20,000.

54) August 6, 1970: Mercantile Bank - $20,000.

55) August 19, 1970: Branch of the Bank of Silver - $12,000.

56) August 19, 1970: Stores the Magician - $28,000.

57) September 10, 1970: Industrial Plant of Esso Standard Oil - $7,000.

58) September 16, 1970: Chalk Factory National - $4,000.

59) September 18, 1970: Company FLEISCHMANN - $800.

60) September 18, 1970: Security truck of the First National City Bank – unknown amount

61) November 17, 1970: Textile mill and a paper plant - $8,000.

62) November 29, 1970: Offices of ACODIKE - $8,000. Kidnap in addition to the Treasurer of the signature.

63) December 1, 1970: YMCA - $20,000.

64) January 15, 1971: Branch bank in the city of Florida - $16,000.

65) February 3, 1971: Unemployment compensation fund US$ 100,000.

66) February 11, 1971: Exchange Branch - $16,000.

67) May 3, 1971: "Remeseros" Bank - $25,600.

68) July 6, 1971: Headquarters of the Magistrates Court of Montevideo - $15,000.

69) September 28, 1971: Coca Cola of Salto City - $2,703.

70) October 1, 1971: Autonomous Local Board - $1,350.

71) October 11, 1971: "The magician": $4,053.

72) November 1, 1971: CUTCSA (urban bus company) - $27,027.

73) November 3, 1971: Credit Bank of the City of Florida - $37,837.

74) November 15, 1971: Casino Park Hotel US$ 46,622.

75) March 8, 1972: Trade located in Gil Street NO. 871 - $122,416.

76) March 15, 1972: Office of UTE (National Electric Company) - $1,000.

77) March 17, 1972: Trade located in the Street. July 18th No.885 - $500.

78) March 23, 1972: Hotel located in the Boulevard Spain No. 2297 - $100.

79) April 6, 1972: Offices of MOORE McCormack, Uruguay - $350.

80) April 7, 1972: a collector of UTE - $400.

81) May 4, 1972: Private home - $45,000.

82) May 17, 1972: Transport company located in Montevideo - $2,700.

83) May 25, 1972: Private home - $12,000.

84) May 26, 1972: Two individual farms - $160,000.

85) June 1972: Three robberies reported - $170,000.

86) In July of 1972: Six thefts result in $1,423.

87) August 1972: 14 robberies that bring them $8,000 in cash and $8,400 in checks.

Stolen weapons

It is important to remember that the main supply of weapons, explosives, logistics, etc. of terrorist groups, both in Uruguay and around the world, came from the Soviet Union it's proxy in the western hemisphere, Cuba. In the framework of the Cold War, the USSR promoted, encouraged and financed terrorism actions of left around the world. The theft of weapons and explosives from different places was also a means of supply.

1. July 31, 1963: theft by the MLN - 33 rifles and 3,700 projectiles, Shooting Club Swiss, most of which had been loaned by the National Army.

2. January 1, 1964: theft by the MLN - 11 rifles and 8 bayonets.

3. April 19, 1964: theft of explosive material at" Cerro Blanco", State of Lavalleja.

4. April 20, 1964: theft of 5 rifles, 6 revolvers and 1,000 projectiles.

5. April 25, 1964: theft of three hundred pounds of explosives of the National Cement Company.

6. February 5, 1965: theft of an armory in the Street Galicia, Montevideo.

7. April 19, 1965: theft of explosive material at "Cerro Blanco", State of Lavalleja.

8. April 2, 1965: theft of 5 rifles, 6 revolvers and 1,000 projectiles.

10. November 27, 1966: theft of 63 weapons, and 10,000 rounds of ammo, and 4 police uniforms of the State of Police were accessed from the armory through a gaping hole.

11. February 18, 1966: theft by the MLN - 10 rifles with fixed bayonets and 18 military uniforms.

12. January 1, 1968: theft of 250 pounds of explosives.

13. November 25, 1968: theft of 100 pounds of gelignite (explosive material, 1 pound is enough to kill a person).

14. April 19, 1971: performed a series of thefts of weapons owned by Dr. Armando Mutter, Mr. Javier Pietropintoy and Mr. Ricardo Rimini, among others.

Attacks

Attacks with explosives and arson (some more powerful and other milder) against private homes, businesses, embassies and media have been a common practice of the terrorists.

1. On 9 September, 1964, in retaliation for the rupture of relations with Cuba, several armed groups throw firebombs at the offices of the City Bank and the maritime company "Moore & McCormack".

2. September 9, 1964: drop bombs of tar against a local Coca Cola company.

3. On 10 September, 1964, the residences of four Government councilors are subject to attacks using Molotov cocktails.

4. September 10, 1964: an explosive device detonated in the studies of Radio Carve.

5. September 10, 1964: an incendiary bomb explodes in the garden of the residence of the Ambassador of Brazil in Montevideo.

6. On 8 December, 1964, again another high-power bomb explodes in front of the offices of the American shipping company Moore McCormack. On the interior walls of the building, persons responsible for action were painted with tar "Gringos Pirates".

7. January 12, 1965: bombing of the offices of propaganda center of Brazil.

8. May 4, 1965: several incendiary bombs are thrown at the Coca Cola factory and against the International Harvester Co.

9. May 5, 1965: arson attack on the General Electric Company.

10. May 5, 1965: arson attack on the Colgate Palmolive Company.

11. On 6 May, 1965, several explosive devices are launched against buildings housing cable companies of American and Western Telegraph.

12. August 9, 1965: bomb attack by the MLN against deposits of the Bayer.

13. October 18, 1965: attacks with bombs to the houses of Mario Heber, president of the Chamber of Deputies, and Alberto Heber, a member of the National Council of Government.

14. December 9, 1965: pump against the home of a leader of the Commercial Camera.

15. December 9, 1965: bomb attack by the MLN against the Chamber of Commerce of Montevideo.

16. December 9, 1965: bomb attack against the home of the President of the Association of Exporters.

17. September 15, 1966: bomb attack against the plant SADREP.

18. October 9, 1966: bomb attack against the home of Colonel Mario Aguerrondo.

19. November 15, 1966: bomb attack against the home of the Sub-Secretary of the Interior.

20. April 11, 1967: bomb attack against the company Burroughs.

21. On 20 June 1967, arson by Tupamaro command at General Motors factory in response to visit of Nelson Rockefeller, producing damage amounting to 250 million pesos, about One million U.S. Dollars. The operation was carried out in the early morning hours by several uniformed policemen, who connected a hose with a truck full of gasoline.

22. September 14, 1967: attack on Radio Carve.

23. On 16 September, 1967 were released four tar bombs on the headquarters of the Cultural Alliance Uruguay- USA.

24. January 23, 1968:a homemade bomb explodes in entrance hall of the building of the Consulate of the United States.

25. April 1, 1968: while in Punta del Este the Conference of American Presidents, with the presence of Lyndon B. Johnson, a high-power bomb explodes in the door of the Uruguayan subsidiary of the American company Burroughs.

26. 1 July, 1968: bombing of the radio station plant Ariel.

27. October 18, 1968: bomb to the Stock Exchange.

28. April 30, 1969: attack with incendiary bombs against COPRIN.

29. June 13, 1969: attack using explosives against the home of the manager of the American company TEM.

30. April 29, 1970: 12 attacks against various offices of U. T. E.

31. September 11, 1970: attack on Coca Cola bottling plant.

32. September 14, 1970: a command of the MLN-T assaults and sets fire to the textile company SUDAMTEX. It is estimated that 3 million meters of fabric and five million U.S. dollars were lost.

33. September 16, 1970: attack with incendiary bombs against offices of International Harvester.

34. October 8, 1970: bomb attack against the firms Coca Cola, Pan American and General Electric.

35. 1 December ,1970: bombing of the host plant of International Telegraph & Telephone Co.

36. September 29, 1970: bomb attack against the Bowling of Carrasco; in action kill the caregiver of the humble place: Hilaria Ibarra.

37. October, 1970: attacks on the electronic equipment of the bowling Zum Zum, IPUSA, and the La Rochelle Restaurant.

38. January 16, 1971: six bombs were planted in the house of Mario Berembau -

39. June 7, 1971: second attack on the home of rector Oscar Maggiolo, and first against the home of Arturo Ardao.

40. August 4, 1971: pumps in the central of the Union and Colorada y Batllista (Colorado Party).

41. December 22, 1971: a Tupamaro command burns down headquarters of Club de Golf de Punta Carretas.

42. December 26, 1971: an explosive device was placed in the house of Daniel Mignon, President of the Guild of Teachers.

43. January 11, 1976: bomb attack to Punta del Este (night club and port of Punta del Este, the last neutralized).

Kidnappings

1. September 9, 1969: Banker and member of the Board of Directors of the company SEUSA, editor of the daily "Morning" and "El Diario" Gaetano Pellegrini Giampietro, released 72 days later by paying a ransom.

2. July 28, 1970: the Judge of Counsel of Instruction, Daniel Pereira Manelli, is kidnapped. The next day a statement is broadcast stating that "the revolutionary courts" began to act and that the judge would be questioned forty-eight hours on "judicial irregularities" in the proceedings against several seditious. He is released on August 4.

3. July 31, 1970: American official of the Technical Assistance of the Chief of Police of Montevideo Anthony Dan Mitrione is kidnapped. He is executed on August 10.

4. July 31, 1970: kidnapping of Brazilian consul and first secretary of the Brazilian ambassador Aloysio Days Gomide. He was released on 21 February, 1971 in exchange for a large ransom.

5. August 7, 1970: Through use of fake credentials, Claude Fly, American official employed by the Ministry of Agriculture and Livestock as expert in soils, is kidnapped.

He was released on March 2, 1971 after having a heart attack.

6. August 7, 1970: first abduction of Ulysses Pereira Reverbel who is released 4 days later.

7. January 8, 1971: British ambassador Geoffrey Jackson kidnapped, finally released on September 10 of the same year.

8. March 10, 1971: kidnapping of Guido Watercress Oribe, Prosecutor in Court, to be interrogated by "the people's court" on its performance, released shortly after.

9. March 30, 1971: second hijacking of Ulysses Pereira Reverbel, kidnapped until May 27, 1972 when the Joint Forces found the prison he was held in.

10. April 13, 1971: businessman Ricardo Ferres is taken, released January 28, 1972.

11. May 14, 1971: abducted Carlos Frick Davies, former minister for livestock and agriculture of Uruguay . His time in captivity was extended until May 27 of 1972 when the joint forces discovered the prison of the town where he was being held.-

12. June 23, 1971: kidnapping of FUNSA Chairman, Dr. Alfredo Cambon who was released three days later.

13. July 12, 1971: kidnapped businessman Jorge Mario Berembau, director of the textile company Hytesa; released on November 26, after paying ransom.

14. August 17, 1971: kidnapped by Dr. Carlos Maeso, broker in the kidnapping of Jorge Berenbau. He was released after 2 days.

15. August 18, 1971: the PRO-33 abducts businessman Luis Fernandez Lladó, manager of the refrigerator Model. He was released on October 8.

16. October 23, 1971: Jose Pereira Gonzalez, co-director of the journal "The Day", is kidnapped and released 5 days later-.

17. February 12, 1972: abducted Homer Farina, editor of the newspaper Action; released on February 29.

18. February 24, 1972: Police photographer Nelson Bardesio is kidnapped and held in the self-styled prison "The Star" (Montevideo). He was subjected to interrogation under duress in order to extract information and released May 5.

19. March 11, 1972: Sergio Molaguero, the son of an entrepreneur in a shoe factory of Santa Lucia, is kidnapped, tortured and kept in captivity for about 70 days.

20. July 28, 1972: 24-hour kidnap by the Manager of United Press International (UPI), Mr. Hector Menoni.

Attempted kidnappings

On July 31, 1970, Michael Gordon Jones, second secretary of the embassy of the United States, was bound hand and feet, wrapped and tied in a blanket, transferred in a pick-up from which the victim was thrown to the pavement, bruised and battered and not able to ask for help. On the same date, the PRO-33 attempted a kidnapping for ransom of Ignacio Parpar, Manager of the Fabrica Nacional de Beer, but failed due to the victim's resistance.

Attempt to hijack of Businessman Juan José Gari by Tupamaros wearing police uniforms on April 21, 1971.

On May 14, 1971, the kidnapping of the industrial Alfredo Raul Deambrosis fails.

Murders

1. Seraphim Billoto Tamaneo, while participating in an act of repudiation against the communist revolution in Cuba. - 10/01/61

2. Oscar Alonso Pombo, a worker, not to abide by a strike of the tobacco trade union. - 1/02/61

3. Dora Isabel Lopez, nursing student, killed by a group led by Raul Sendic in the assault and fire to the Confederation of Trade Unions of Uruguay by discrepancies with the signature of a convention. - 05/05/62

4. Police Commissioner Antonio Silveira died in procedure.- 27/12/66

5. Sergeant Second Class Enrique Fernandez Diaz - 19/01/69

6. Agent Juan Francisco De Garay Lamasok, while trying to stop the theft of his weapon. - 08/07/69

7. Agent (Retired.) Manuel Tejera - 29/07/69

8. Carlos Rodriguez , the taking of Pando. - 08/10/69

9. Agent Juan Antonio Viera Piazza - 12/11/69

10. Agent Carlos Ruben Zembrano Rivero - 15/11/69
11. Agent Juan Manuel Tejera Bobadilla - 29/12/69
12. Agent Alfredo Pallas Cardozo - 13/02/70
13. Police Inspector Hector Moran Charquero - 13/04/70
14. Asunción Pérez de Mello Aidiz - 3/06/70
15. Armando Lesses Agent Alvarez - 05/07/70
16. Dan Mitrione - 10/08/70 (American Citizen abducted on 31/07/70)
17. Agent Nelson Esteban Machado Carreño - 19/08/70
18. Hilaria Ibarra, an employee of the Bowling of Carrasco, killed by bomb explosion. - 29/09/70
19. José Leandro Villalba - 11/01/71
20. Agent Nelson Sinbad Sosa Fernandez - 1/02/71
21. Richard George Brown - 5/02/71
22. Agent Gilberto Carballo Gonzalez - 21/04/71
23. Metropolitan Guard Aidis Pérez was murdered by a Tupamaro command from another car - 03/06/71
24. Metropolitan Guard Walter Custodian Rodriguez - 22/06/71.
25. Juan Andres Betancourt , night watch employee, murdered while giving notice to the police of theft in the company. - 22/06/71
26. Metropolitan Guard Miguel Zubiri - 07/27/71
27. Ildefonso Kaulaukas, executed. - 30/07/71
28. Alfonso Arhancet, 15-year-old boy who threw paint at a local of the Broad Front, was persecuted, brutally beaten and shot dead.- 7/08/71

29. Agent Juan Alvarez in the attack on the supermarket "Manzanarez". - 11/08/71

30. Republican Guard Wilder Daniel Soto Romero was murdered in custody of the Hospital Pedro Visca - 02/09/71

31. Republican Guard Nelson Lima Gutierrez murdered in custody of the Hospital Pedro Visca - 02/09/71

32. Sergeant Santos Alcides Ferreira Chavez - 15/10/71

33. Agent Mª Juan Antonio Fernández - 26/11/71

34. Pascasio Baez Mena, 35 year-old farm worker - 29/12/71

35. Police Cadet Heber Washington Castiglioni - 19/01/72

36. Inspector Rodolfo Leoncino - 27/01/72

37. Agent Juan González, in Tupamaro attempt to take his Police Station - 28/01/72

38. Agent Rosibel Do Canto, while traveling on his motorcycle. - 13/02/72

39. Officer Juan Manuel Sanchez - 13/02/72

40. Agent Segundo Fernandez - 13/02/72

41. Carlos Maria Iturria - 24/03/72

42. Sub Commissioner Oscar Luzardo - 04/14/72.

43. Police Officer Carlos Alberto Leites - 04/14/72.

44. Captain Ernesto Motto Benvenuto - 04/14/72

45. Professor Armando Acosta and Lara - 04/14/72

46. Captain Wilfredo Busconi - 17/04/72

47. Soldier Luis Alberto Nuñez - 20/04/72

48. Dr. Julio Federico Morato , murdered in his home by those trying to steal surgical material. - 04/05/72

49. Soldier Saul Diaz - 18/05/72

50. Soldier Osiris Núñez Silva - 18/05/72

51. Soldier Gaudencio Núñez Santiago - 18/05/72

52. Soldier Ramon Ferreira Escobal - 18/05/72

53. Soldier Eusebio Rodriguez - 15/06/72

54. Aurora Rodriguez de Abreu - 16/06/72

55. Soldier Adhemair Victor Aguilar - 23/06/72

56. Soldier Eduardo Delgado - 23/06/72

57. Vicente Jaime Oloza Garcia, bus driver - murdered for refusing to take the vehicle to escape. - 28/06/72

58. Diego Romulo Terra Olivera, merchant confused with a politician. - 28/06/72

59. Policeman Luis José Barbizan, murdered in his home. - 03/07/72

60. Agent Luciano Ismael Conde - 09/07/72

61. Captain Roberto Botta Truncheon - 19/07/72

62. Colonel Artigas Gregorio Alvarez Armelino - 25/07/72

63. Official Darwin Fernandez - 08/17/72

64. Lt.(Army) Ricardo Lysimachus Braida Matalonga - 08/18/72

65. José Luis López Gómez - 28/08/72

66. Agent Sagunto Goni - 03/22/73 (wounded 14/04/72)

67. Carlos Luis Quieto Rickeboer - 08/18/73

68. Captain Wilfredo Busconi - 31/01/74

69. Soldier Nelson Viqueque - 1/04/74
70. Sergeant Artigas Maya - 3/04/74
71. Manuel Areosa - 6/04/74
72. Julio C Bremerman - 21/04/74
73. Guidet Cesar Dotti - 26/10/74
74. Roberto Raul Gonzalez - 29/10/74
75. Colonel Ramon Trabal Usera - 19/12/74
76. Carlos Abdala - 8/06/76

Countries that supported the terrorists in Uruguay

1 - USSR
 a - training courses: political – subversive.
 b – Military training courses.
 c - Courses on falsification of documents.
 d - Communications courses and courses of armament.
 f - Provision of money.

2 - CZECHOSLOVAKIA
 a - Provision of false identity documents.
 b - Point of change/documents for travellers
 c - Provision of arms under legal form.

3 - REPUBLIC OF CUBA.
 a - Support for the formation of Uruguayan terrorist column in its territory.
 b - Military training courses for conventional war.

c - Military training courses for irregular warfare and insurrection.

d - Courses of falsification of documents of all types.

e - Communications courses.

f - Provision of arms, munitions and other war equipment.

g - Sent to Uruguay of supervisors for the terrorist and subversive activity.

4 - REPUBLIC OF CHILE (Under Salvador Allende)

a- Support for the formation of a Uruguayan terrorist column in its territory.

b - Formed in point of supply of weapons, munitions and war material.

c - Formed its government in nexus between terrorist groups and the Government of Cuba.

Chapter 6

The Absence

For most children, some events pass unnoticed while others do not. Unless their circumstances are extreme, children live their lives distracted by their immediate surroundings. They are usually unaware of the things in the larger world beyond. I believe this to be a divine protection against the damage caused by painful experiences and setbacks of childhood. Sometimes the adults entrusted to protect you fail to do so. That is when the painful experiences have a much easier time finding you.

In my home there were now only the two of us. My mother was forced to put my father in the past yet for some time he remained her drug, her elixir, her true love. With his departure, that relationship was abruptly gone. I think she held on as long as she could but was under intense pressure. She eventually decided she had to start over again. We remained alone through some difficult times. It was slightly easier for me. I remained living in the same house, playing on the same sidewalks with the same friends on the same streets. As time passed memories of my father became more and more distant. They faded and most seemed to disappear in the mists of time. Now other faces and figures quickly became more important.

My grandmother, Maria Emilia, became my rock. She was there in the hospital the night I was born. According to her, my first year was tiring for everyone. Rarely does a newborn arrive weighing 12 pounds! On top of that, I was given to crying and was very restless. My grandmother was always there. Maria Emilia was persistent and she stayed despite my mother's resentments as I found out much later.

My two favorite uncles were also there when I was born. Gustavo was fourteen and the younger brother of my mother. Justo was about thirty and my father's younger brother. They were both artists and I still have memories of how they both constantly swirled in and out and around in my life.

Uncle Justo was a famous singer. He always came by on his motorcycle to pick me up to go enjoy family gatherings. We shared the same birthday during the winter which made it a great occasion to share hot chocolate and other treats. I still remember being delighted with his guitars and his unique singing voice.

Uncle Gustavo was a cartoonist and painter from an early age. He was a teenager when I was born. I loved it when he took me fishing or when we just stayed home to enjoy movies together. We both liked the faded look of black and white films on our old television.

Outside my childhood world, I was ignorant that a different world was forming. By that time the military dictatorship had come to power and the Tupamaros were mostly defeated. Many were in prisons and others escaped Uruguay to hide in other countries. Meantime, my mother was devoted to her work, always trying to find a new business opportunity. Meantime, I found refuge in my toys and with my friends in the neighborhood. My devotion to books and writing also started from early age. And for some reason, I also fell in love with sunsets.

My mother was twenty-six when I was born and thirty-one when my father left for Paraguay. When she decided to start over, she began seeing a medical student a few years younger than she was. He was a second-generation Middle Eastern man. His family was from Lebanon and had emigrated here after the war.

In the beginning it was not bad. I was a kid and he seemed to me like a new adult friend. He was finishing his medical degree in Montevideo, so he wasn't around very often. In the early years they were together, things continued much unchanged for me. My family was changing but my life still had not changed much. My school had a dress code that was strongly enforced. Boys wore short hair, not touching the collar of their shirt. The girls also had rules regarding their hair and clothing. I was educated in patriotism, about the heroes of our independence movement, and I gained respect for our national symbols. The strict schools where the main reason Uruguay become one of the best-educated societies in Latin America.

As a child, the military dictatorship did not represent anything to me. But its reality in everyday life meant that for the most part, we didn't live in a democracy anymore. Freedom of the press, freedom of association and assembly, free expression – all were closely monitored and disrupted if they deviated from support for the regime.

As time went by, the military commanders became more radical. The focus of their witch hunts really expanded. No longer were they coming just for the Tupamaro terrorists. Now anyone who opposed the regime in any way became a target. Thus began another dark period in Uruguay, with disappearances, imprisonment, torture, and new blacklists. The military movement was also supported by a new breed of ultra-radical politicians. Both were paranoid and kept up the hunt for an invisible enemy.

My stepfather had become a doctor and had been hired to work as for the military. People who knew him wondered over the years what exactly his tasks were behind the walls of the military base. Many have speculated his medical training was being used more to gain confessions and information for the military and not so much for regular practice of medicine.

My last name also began to bring me trouble at school. I was now known as the young son of an overthrown politician. Even though my father left the country to protect us from the abuse by association, the stigma remained.

My last name also brought me difficulty at home as well. There, I was the young son of an absent father whose mother had now become obsessed with removing all traces of him from our lives. Getting rid of the reminders and keepsakes was not enough. She started a new crusade with the goal of changing my name. This was the last connection I had to my father, and the last concrete reminder to her of his existence. As a minor I had no say in the process and I fought it every way I could. The process took years to complete. Even my original birth certificate disappeared. Much to my mother's satisfaction, she was finally able to wipe almost all official records of my father from our lives.

My new name brought many other changes. On paper, my stepfather became my father. This gave him certain rights and freedoms in the eyes of the military bosses. He was now free to use techniques on me he had practiced behind those military base walls. Physical abuse and punishment became a common occurrence in my life. Discipline was always taught with physical punishment as the consequence for failure. It was brutal. Here I was, a 100-pound kid trying to defend myself against a 6-foot, 250-pound monster.

I am going to share two things in reference to this: I was forced each year by him to sign a document he wrote at the start of classes. It established the physical punishment I would receive for each school supply I would lose. A pencil lost was a fist to my face, an eraser was a punch in my stomach, and on it went. The second thing is that many of the brutal beatings I received at the hands of my "paper father" was quietly observed by my mother. I remember as she stood at my bedroom door watching as this monster beat me. She never protested or spoke out.

There was one particular beating I can still see vividly remember. I remember being in my room, lying on the floor and face up. From where I lay, I could look at the ceiling and see where it was splattered with my own blood. My facial swelling from the beating lasted for several days. I was forced to lie to others that I had fallen from my bike. I was ten years old and barely 100 pounds. After repeated blows, , my mother finally said, "Enough, Enough!"

I can still see the horror in the face of my grandmother when she saw me the next morning. To her credit, she never believed the story of an accident with my bike. I remember as she confronted my parents harshly. I silently worried that it would result in worse for me. The abuse continued and my stepfather started to draw more on his military interrogation training. The physical punishment he imposed became more devious. I recall his technique of wrapping a wet towel around his fists. He then directed the blows to the soft parts of my body so as not to leave surface bruises and marks.

Sometimes after his beatings, I reacted by running out of the house. On occasion, I ran to the nearby to the police station. On my last trip there, the police held me as he was summoned to the station. He called another doctor to examine me in front of them. While I lifted my t-shirt he said, "OK, show the doctor the marks." The doctor who examined me was another military doctor, a buddy of his, and they worked together on the military base. His friend covered for him and nothing ever came of it. Now I knew which side the police were on. Who knows what other atrocities they shared and hid for each other?

For many years I planned in my mind how I was going to destroy this monster, dwelling on how I was going to make him pay for the pain and injustice he inflicted upon me. Did I follow through with my plan for revenge? The answer is no, I did not. I realized he was not worth me ruining my life any further by exacting my revenge and getting caught. His solid place in the military meant the deck was heavily stacked against me.

Last I knew he still enjoyed a good reputation as a doctor. He became State Representative for Soriano in the National Party of Uruguay. He was also the President of the Lebanese Club. As far as I know, he never paid for his abuse of me, at least not yet. I never gave up hope that I could escape this hell. I tried and failed many times, but I never gave up. Never once did I think about taking my own life.

I know while I tell my story, there are other children who receive the same abuse or worse. I would like to share this message, our message:

> *There is always hope, always an outlet. Perhaps it is not apparent, so keep trying. Keep looking for the exit, and never give up! Please do not fill your heart with hatred and revenge. Do not do to others what they did to you.*

I am not a psychologist or an expert, but I am a survivor. I feel no shame in denouncing this man's abuse. Always remember you cannot allow the abuse you received to make you an abuser. Do not let yourself down. I was finally able to break free from this pain of my past, but it cost me a great deal of time working through the misery. The physical wounds healed relatively quickly, but the emotional wounds of the soul do not heal as fast or as well, even less when bitterness and revenge take us down other roads. Never believe that the abuse is your fault or its because you are not good enough. It happens because they are monsters.

When I returned to school for my second year with my new name, someone had made the mistake of trying to cut into line by using my old last name. I returned home to tell my mother. In those days we lived in a two-story house that had two sets of stairs. The internal one led to the second-floor bedrooms. The external stairs extended from the rear terrace to the patio. I came down using the external stairs and entered the dining room while my mother was on the phone with her back turned to me. I heard her say: "...after all the brainwashing we have done - this brings it all back." The horrible error at school that morning of using my old name meant that her master plan to erase my father from my mind had still not succeeded. To my credit, it never would.

As I reflect, I am still amazed that the brutal physical abuse at the hands of my stepfather and the psychological abuse from my mother did not make me an abuser as well. I did become very rebellious but along the way, I kept the tender heart of my father. It was like I had put on a breastplate to protect myself in order to survive a little longer in search of the truth. I do not wish to acknowledge all my mistakes but they did not turn my heart dark. What I did not know is that in the future I would lose my compass for a time. I would be lost in the sea of life, without rudder, without hatred, but still full of pain.

During this period of struggle in my live, the military regime was starting to lose its grip on the country. My father returned from Paraguay but restrictions on his liberty were imposed. This did not keep him from violating those restrictions by exercising his right of free speech. He was detained for this and jailed several times. After being released, he continued by example to lead others on the pathway back to democracy.

All over the country, the political world and our country was undergoing many changes but my life as a boy had mostly remained much the same. My only refuge was to escape for a few days to the home of my maternal grandmother.

Hers was an old house, not very large, but with a huge back yard I loved. It was filled with a variety of plants and banana trees. It was my safe place and my hiding place. Going to Grandma's house transported me to another world. For hours I listened to her stories. She recounted tales of her childhood in the field, of the harshness of farm life, and always stories of her brothers and sisters. My grandmother had suffered economic poverty most of her life. I think she and I learned to flee the poverty using her imagination to visit better places. I loved it best at bedtime. I would listen spellbound as she told more stories that fueled my imagination.

Harshness of life had also taught her how to save. As frugal as she was, she even looked for ways to save more. The last few times I got to visit her she cooked dinner in the dark, only illuminated by the flame of the stove. With the arrival of color television years later, she complained for days how much electrical energy the red light on the front of the television must be using throughout the night! My grandmother was the great statesman of the household. She taught us how important it was that we all master our responsibilities so we could carry them out to perfection and with proper attitudes.

Her husband was a police officer who retired before I could even walk. He was very formal and not easy to approach. Whenever I visited him, he was present but it was as if he was not. He lived a hard childhood. It was probably harder even than mine but those periods of his life had been locked away in long-forgotten vaults of the past, in trunks that he never opened. I have only a few memories of him, but they were all pleasant.

When I was eleven years old, my grandfather decided to end his life. We can only guess what caused him to do so. I just remember that one Sunday, he just jumped from the bridge near his home. I was never able to discover why and will probably never know. Neither will I judge him. Somehow his death cemented in me the determination that I would never end my life this way. I know that the human mind has convoluted ways. It is easily deluded and it is difficult to understand.

Through his death, my grandfather became one more name on the list of people I needed, but who became absent from my life. In a strange way his final gift was to confirm to me that the way he chose to end things would not ever be for me.

After the death of my grandfather, my grandmother would visit my house every Wednesday. For me it was a great relief to see her. We talked for endless hours and often played cards. We shared the same room so were able to continue the stories until the late hours of the night.

Her house was two miles away, and but she insisted on walking it every Wednesday so we could have a snack and our time together. On this particular Wednesday, I waited anxiously for her to arrive. I assumed she was late so I went to run some errands. I returned home later that day to find the house was still empty.

That would be the last day I would see my grandmother in our house. My mother resented her relationship with me so she decided Grandmother could not visit anymore or have any contact with me. After my name was changed, my mother also started to limit my contact with my Uncle Justo as well. He was one of the few who had stayed around while I was growing up.

So, yet another door was closed that day. Without Grandmother and Uncle Justo, my circle definitely grew smaller. It was now mostly populated by people on my stepfather's side. Even while claiming a place as my uncles, and grandparents, they were nothing more than strangers, outsiders. My life became a nightmare, a life to which one wakes up daily and finds it is a lie. I was still a kid and increasingly isolated from the ones I loved.

Life continued to move along. Uncle Gustavo, who often had taken me to fish on the bank of the river, had grown up and married. The year was 1984 and I was just turning 13. Democracy began peeking out of hiding once again. People put campaign signs in the streets once more. My father became a candidate for the Senate for the Colorado Party. Uncle Gustavo, with a long tradition in the Colorado Party, hung a red poster with black letters in defiance of the government that read simply:

District 5-40
Pozzolo
Senator

My father won, and his victory awakened the flames of rancor in my mother. She decided this time to make her case against his brother. In this way Uncle Gustavo became the latest traitor in the eyes of my mother.

Through all this family drama, I learned to build my own worlds in my imagination. I learned to dream as a way to dig my way out from the psychological prison created by my mother and stepfather. While I was still a minor, I decided to escape from my house. I remember my first girlfriend, Amy, an American born in Des Moines, Iowa. She helped me to move my clothes from my mother's house to the home of a family friend who had agreed to take me in, the Saenz family.

Amy had come to Uruguay for a cultural exchange program with the United States. She remained in Uruguay for only one year. We shared eleven months of close friendship. She helped me with my English for hours and we often walked along the bank of the river. When she returned to the U.S. in July 1986, I fell into a tremendous depression; it was as if the air in my lungs had vanished. For weeks I was lying in a dark room, trying to understand why yet another door had closed so soon after it had opened. Somehow, this door hurt so much more than the others. The separation burned as if it were acid in my veins.

I lay in that borrowed bed, without a family I could trust, without a clear future, without direction, and with no idea how to dump the heavy sack of emotions I was carrying. I was tired and sick of all of it. What I did not know was that these experiences – all the pain and challenges - was only just the beginning of a tour about to become more difficult in ways I could not imagine.

Chapter 7

U-boats in South America

Along with our keepsakes from my father, his library of hundreds of books about freedom and democracy disappeared. I found out later that these books had also been burned by my mother during her attempt to purge all trace of my father from our lives. Curiously, during this period of hatred and persecution, my mother's own library was growing. Her choices were heavily focused on Nazi books and other fascist publications. She proudly exhibited a book written by Adolf Hitler titled, <u>My Struggle</u>. Most Americans know this book as <u>Mein Kampf</u>.

Many Uruguayan military personnel were still pro-Nazi years after WW II. It was reported that the interior offices of some of the country's military bases proudly displayed the Nazi flag with a swastika. Anti-Semitism became another obsession for my mother. She had somehow transformed into a monster of neo-Nazism. She practiced old Nazi customs like looking at the shape of people's noses, the position of their ears, the shape of the skull as a method of exposing Jewish people. Fortunately, I did not inherit her hatred toward the Jewish race or any other ethnic group.

Regardless of her motivation, the Nazis still exerted a great influence in South America after World War II and in the decades that followed. The origin of this very likely had to do with agreements that were struck with Third Reich officials around the time of the German surrender. Two Argentine investigators would later make an extraordinary contribution to unveil what has been called the last secret operation of World War II. Their investigation revealed with almost certainty that several operations were implemented under the umbrella of the British Government that facilitated the escape of high Nazi officials from the heavy Soviet fist of Communism. Their destination was primarily the countries of Argentina and Uruguay.

It appears that at least five German U-boats reached Argentina with no less than fifty high-ranking Third Reich officials. A great deal of looted gold was also rumored to be on board. WWII ended on May 7, 1945. The first submarine arrived in Argentina on July 10, 1945. A second sub arrived later that same year on August 17. Upon arrival, the German U-boats each of the surrendered to the Argentine Navy.

The U-boat commanders were arrested and interrogated in Buenos Aires, Washington and London. It was learned that while in transit, they had sunk the USS Battleship Eagle 56 and the Brazilian cruiser Bahia. The resulting death toll was more than 400, including U.S. citizens. Both the U.S. and British governments subsequently covered up the operation. Why would the British and the Americans hide the deaths of more than 400 people after the war had ended two months earlier?

There are several theories about this but the most likely suggests that the safe passage and arrival of these Nazi officials was the result of a conspiracy whose goal was to stop the advance of Stalin's troops in Europe. For that operation to succeed, it required the involvement of key German officers and soldiers to remain in Europe to assist in the fight against Stalin. Some stayed to help the Allies while others were permitted to slip away without repercussions. Many also choose to resettle in South America. The officers who remained Europe probably stayed in exchange for the escape of their families. Perhaps they cooperated with the expectation of joining them later. Unfortunately for them, the outcry for Nazi war criminals to be brought to justice made it likely that few ever escaped.

Many of those Third Reich high officials ultimately found cover in the sparsely populated southern regions of

Argentina and Chile. If true, it makes it easy to understand why Argentine Patagonia has one of the largest German communities in Latin America. That community also includes the direct descendants of many Nazi war criminals. It has also been speculated that Adolf Hitler may also have been a passenger on one of these U-boats. Perhaps Stalin's suspicions that Hitler had actually fled either to Argentina or Spain might have been true.

Many countries in post-WWII South America were already ruled by fascist-style military dictatorships. It is easy to see why they would have welcomed the brutal servants of Nazism into their ranks with few questions asked. The incorporation of these Third Reich refugees into the military organizations was swift and widespread.

My stepfather had a very close relationship to the military regime while they were in power. Many of them held a deep belief in the methods of violence and the hatred that drove the Third Reich. Had some of these Nazis or their friends infiltrated my family and brainwashed my mother? Where did she get the books on Nazism which I saw in my house? Perhaps this is why the destructive fascination for Nazism became a part of her very being. I will never know.

Chapter 8

Operation Condor

Operation Condor was a plan between several Latin American countries throughout the 1970's and 1980's to eliminate political dissidents. It quickly became a coordinated campaign that eventually involved all of the South American military dictatorships. The speed in which it was implemented suggests the plan was guided by some unseen third party. Eventually they were all sharing information and tactics to track, kidnap and kill people they had labelled terrorists. Almost everyone could qualify - trade unionists, left-wing militants, students, clergy, journalists, guerrillas. Frequently, the families of the declared dissidents were used as pawns to crush or silence them.

It would eventually be confirmed that the Condor plan grew out of a CIA-backed effort to contain and control the opponents of the CIA's allies in South America. The CIA's goal was to promote the stability of regimes friendly to

America. Human rights or civil liberties were rarely a consideration. Condor was first adopted by the Chilean dictator Augusto Pinochet in November, 1975. Evidence of this would only come to light decades later to confirm that Condor was supported by U.S. Secretary of State Henry Kissinger from its inception.

The exact number of deaths directly attributed to Operation Condor is disputed. Some estimate at least 60,000 and possibly more. Condor's key members were the governments of Argentina, Chile, Uruguay, Paraguay, Bolivia and Brazil. The United States provided technical support and even direct military assistance from the program's inception until Republican Ronald Reagan closed it down after becoming President in 1981.

In June 1999, by order of President Bill Clinton, the U.S. State Department declassified and released thousands of additional documents. It was revealed for the first time in detail that the CIA and the Departments of State and Defense were intimately aware and supported Operation Condor. One Department of Defense intelligence report dated October 1, 1976 noted that Latin American military officers actually bragged about the complicity between the participants and their U.S. counterparts.

Operation Condor cast a very wide net. Without due process in any form, that net also swept up many innocent people who ended up in prisons or worse. Many others died at the hands of the military. It was a classic justification using the rationale that the ends justify the means. The military dictatorship controlling Uruguay at the time went to great lengths under Operation Condor to make sure that the Tupamaros movement was disarmed and defeated. Those who were not caught fled to neighboring countries. Many took refuge in Europe and Mexico.

Operation Condor also ran parallel to my mother's own obsession with removing the last traces of my father from our lives that I referred to in a previous chapter. I still remember that manic evening where all the gifts from him, all of our photographs together, anything physical to link him to our lives went up in the smoke in a mountain of fire in our backyard. She burned everything she could get her hands on. I would find out later that his entire personal library also fell victim to her purge.

Chapter 9

A New Door

One Saturday evening in June, a knock was heard against a massive gray wooden door of a century-old building that had once housed a local newspaper. The door was opened and a man entered. The building was now the headquarters of the Colorado Party. The building was filled with people, as was the tiled sidewalk along the entire block.

I was also heading to that same building. I had to navigate through a packed sea of faces and finally reached that same door on that cold winter evening. When I knocked, the door slowly opened to reveal a dimly lit lobby. Standing in the middle of the room was the man. He stood there in a shimmering gray suit. I stood there in disbelief. It was as if my feet were glued to the floor. Without a word, my father quickly closed the space between us and hugged me for what seemed like forever.

More than a decade had passed since he had left. Tonight, behind that huge door, my father had finally reappeared. His appearance marked the end of the eternity of my childhood without him. I stiffened, not yet able to enjoy the embrace of my father that day. I was no longer a child but a young man who was still bound by hatred, pain, and bitterness. I was like a damaged bird, wanting to fly but unable to so.

I remember we sat in two chairs, one beside the other. My father was now no longer my legal father in the eyes of the courts but that did not matter. I sat silently listening to him, trying to decide which path to follow. He did all the talking. My heart longed to give him a chance but my mind filled with doubt. The ten years of feeling abandoned felt like a freshly-opened wound.

As we sat there, he mapped out a plan for the near future. My father's immediate political schedule required him to give several more interviews. We pondered ways we might spend time together without my mother finding out. Then, too soon, it was the time for me to leave. The gray door opened again and we went out together into the noise of the crowd. My father placed his left arm on my shoulder. We walked through the people and I still remember his gestures and his smile. How I wish I could have been free to enjoy the moment!

As we crossed the street full of people, I wondered if he had meant the hug or was that just one more part of his political propaganda? The inability to accept his friendship and love would continue for some time to bring more pain and darkness as it followed me everywhere like a demon from hell.

The year was 1986. My father had been elected Senator of the Republic the previous year, just after his return from exile. The Colorado Party candidates had quickly won a majority in the elections as Uruguay had left behind the darkness of the military regime. The country was being reborn as a democracy with the election of President Julio Maria Sanguinetti. The newly-free press declared that democracy had reconquered the country. After a decade of domestic terrorism and a dozen years of military rule, the rebirth of this democracy could be felt in the streets. The radio stations, newspapers, and television all flourished once again in the freedom of the press that announced "La Reconquista".

Once again, the people had the freedom to gather and associate openly. The political parties had re-established offices. In the evenings the people were now free gathered to debate and exchange ideas over coffee or a bottle of wine.

Once again families could enjoy a cookout without the fear of the government.

The new democratic government also faced many other problems which were not just economic. When the Colorado Party took power, the Tupamaros were still being held in prisons. Since these individuals were incarcerated without judicial process, the new government decided release them under a grant of amnesty. Military personnel imprisoned during the dictatorship were also given similar immunity. Too late would the reborn democracy's leaders realize their compassion and attempts to foster reconciliation would become the seeds that would lead once more to a Socialist hell.

The captured Tupamaros who had been in prison were now protected from prosecution for their past crimes by the new law. In addition, the worst military perpetrators were also pardoned and could not be tried in court for their offenses. In addition, many of the old Tupamaros who had fled the country as their terror war was crushed began to return. Once again they would be free to live and operate in a new democracy similar to the one they had previously fought to destroy.

During the twelve years of military dictatorship, one thing the regime had been able to do was make many improvements to Uruguay's infrastructure. Unfortunately, it too, was on borrowed money. The new roads and ports also came with a bigger and more impossible international debt. The economic problems from this debt would linger for years while crushing any chances to boost the country's economic growth.

Sadly, this combination of the national amnesty and enormous debt would combine in a terrible way. The aging Tupamaros immediately began to capitalize on the economic problems. They demanded a return to the Socialism that, once embraced, would again crush our fragile democracy. As British Prime Minister Margaret Thatcher would later observe:

"Socialism is great until you run out of other people's money."

However, in the here and now at least, people were thriving in a country where it was possible once again to express thoughts freely. It was an exhilarating feeling which even seemed to make the economic pain easier to bear.

My young life continued to be filled with constant change and confusion while I lived in the home of my friends. When my mother learned of my meeting with my father that day, she forced me to return to her house. I was still a minor so I had no choice. The night I returned we had a meeting between my mother, my "on paper" father, and me. My mother used all her brainwashing tools in an attempt to change my mind, and our meeting dragged on for hours. Finally, my mother drew a line - my real father, or her and the Monster. My stepfather threw his watch on top of the table and said: "You have 15 minutes to make your decision." As they were leaving the dining room I called out, "I have nothing to think about, I'm leaving."

I was gone for about two years with one brief return home. Each time we met, my mother pressured me to renounce my real father and return to live with them. There was no possibility that would work. As I got older, I was becoming more restless and out of control. One fateful night I took my mother's car without permission. I had only driven two blocks before being t-boned by another car. It sent me crashing into a neighborhood bakery. No one else was hurt, but I spent some time in the hospital. The accident was clearly the other driver's fault. I was not drunk but the car was my mother's. Sadly, the accident brought a storm of lies and accusations against me that I did not understand.

I soon realized that my father's opponents were responsible for the turmoil. They were ready and they pounced. These 'attackers of the Black Chief' made political hay with me, his son, even though I was just 18-years-old and not involved in politics.

In those two years before I returned to her house, many things happened. After the reunion meeting with my father, we spent as much time together as possible. He always had a busy political schedule but he was somehow able to make time for us to go hunting, camping, and fishing. We were finally able to spend the quality time together I had longed for as a young boy.

Sadly, during our times together there was still an unspoken wall between us. From the day of our reunion, he continued looking for something in my eyes he couldn't find. In many ways we were like two strangers who could not share a bond of trust. The doubts planted by my mother were powerful and always present. He couldn't see himself in my eyes because I never gave him a chance for that.

My mother refused to give up. Here verbal assaults against my father were exhausting. Even though my father was a Senator, the law was on her side so legally he had no parental rights in the eyes of the court. She continued to push to keep me away from him in any way she could.

Because I would not go back to their home, I was sent to live at the Adventist Institute. It was a boarding school and my first prison. I became more rebellious, more lost, and refused help from anyone. One day while everyone else was in class I pulled my mattress out on to the grass and slept in the middle of the Institute courtyard where everyone could see me. The teachers and pastors could not move me from there.

Even worse was that the Institute served NO meat! They were vegetarians! Seventy percent of the main course diet in Uruguay is beef so I would call my father and ask him to come to pick me up and take me for a steak dinner. Based on the court instructions, he was not permitted to take me away from the Institute. However, my pleading sometimes won out and he did sneak me away a couple of times.

My father always had a great sense of humor. I remember one of the times that he hid me in the back of his station wagon. I was covered with a blanket so he could slip me to a restaurant for a steak. We left the grounds and made good our escape. Leaving to go out to eat some meat and a drink Coke with him was a clear violation of the rules but I didn't care. He called back to the rear of the 'empty' car, "Your mother told the Court that I was a bad influence on you, but I don't know who is the real bad influence here."

During my time at the Institute my mother insisted I was not allowed to leave the property. She made it very clear she was the only one who could take me off the Institute property. So, while I was at the Institute, she came once a month with a family friend and asked if I wanted to go out and I always refused. She never stopped trying to wear me down, but she could not.

The Adventist Institute put up with me for a few months until a few of the female students and I became involved. I'm pretty sure two of the girls thought they were in love with me. Then came the night I was caught trying to climb in to the ladies' dormitory on the second floor over the lunch room. Shortly after that incident, my mother was told I needed to go.

For a short time, I went back to Mercedes to stay with my grandmother. She was living by herself, so we spent time together like we did when I was a kid. My mother never liked the influence Grandma had over me. She quickly found me another 'prison' to attend - the Military High School. This would be another in her long string of unsuccessful challenges to break my spirit.

So here I was once again, 17-years old this time and in another new place. The first night sleeping in the company barracks I could hear some of the kids who had never been away from home crying in the dark, I was already a veteran. To cheer them up, I gathered my recruits that night to instruct them on how to properly conduct a pillow war. Somehow, we managed to break all the lights in the barracks. So, on my second day at the Military High School, I earned two weeks in detention – my own self-imposed prison within a prison.

In spite of the restrictions, I enjoyed the physical part of the military training. I rose to the challenge and pushed myself to the limits. I embraced it all - the combat simulation away from the base, sleeping in tents, shooting guns, tactical training, and sirens awakening us in the middle of the night. I even found a way to benefit from the punishment for the inevitable mistakes. I was now able to pay with pushups and frog jumps instead of weekend detention. This was simple compared to the punishment I received back home as a kid. However, even though my physical performance excelled, my attitude toward authority was terrible and they eventually asked my mother to withdraw me from there as well.

I returned once again to my grandmother's home in Mercedes and from there back to live with my mother. That is when I took her car and had the accident. After I recovered from my injuries, I believe my mother finally realized that her endless war to alienate me from my real father was lost and she soon, finally, left me alone.

Chapter 10

The Black Chief

Luis Bernardo Pozzolo Pica was born in 1933, the eldest of six children. He grew up in extreme poverty in a house without water or electricity. His nights were lit by kerosene lanterns. His father was a federal worker who fell ill in 1940 with tuberculosis. During the next decade, my grandfather was unable to work and the household fell into poverty. In 1950, the TB cure finally came to Uruguay. My father came running and yelling to the house that penicillin would save the life of his father. Sadly, it was not to be. His disease was too advanced and that same year, his father died.

My grandparents were in charge of the cemetery in that part of town. My father and his brothers were able to work helping people by offering them "water and a ladder". The burial sites in the cemeteries in Uruguay are above ground so many widows would not or could not climb the ladder to water or freshen the flowers. My father and his brothers helped to clean the graves, put out new flowers, and run errands in exchange for handouts. This helped a little with the income of the house.

There is a story my uncle told me many times of a widow who had always dealt with my father at the cemetery. Decades later, when my father was a congressman, he recognized the widow in a group of people. He approached and asked: "Water and a ladder?" She looked into his eyes for a few seconds and started to cry once she recognized him.
"So you are that dark- skinned kid from the cemetery! What a beautiful country we now have!"

After his father died, the family's economic situation worsened. However, a new federal law was passed months later that resulted in the position his father had held being offered to him. He came home so excited and happy to tell his mother of the new opportunity.

"What job you will have?" she asked

"Digging holes with a pick and a shovel to install electrical poles." He replied.

She thought about it for a few minutes and said, "No, you were not born to dig holes with a pick and shovel for the rest of your life. You are going to continue with your studies!"

I'm sure that was a very difficult decision. Who knows what our life would have been like had he stayed and taken that job? We will never know. He continued in technical school, learning accounting. He was able later to take a job in banking. In 1962, he was elected Congressman at only 29-years-old. He was re-elected again in 1966. He then won a position in the Senate in 1971, just a few years before the military Coup forced him to leave the country.

My father inherited his passion for public speaking and the courage to tell the truth from his uncle, a street vendor of vegetables who used his gift as a speaker to fight the dictatorship in 1933. My father was a hard-hitting politician, approaching difficult issues head on; his message was full of passion. He remained inspired by his people and was always fighting for their best interests. He was also attacked, mostly by those who 'hidden under the bed' during the military dictatorship.

All along, he and the other like-minded Uruguayan politicians always fought to restore democracy. Because of his tireless efforts to bring back democracy, he was also jailed several times. He had a thick political skin and able to take the punishment of the witch hunts from the left. Because of these shadowed attacks and his dark skin, he earned the name "The Black Chief."

But there was always a price to be paid. In the late 1980's, he endured one of the worst of these slanderous attacks of his career on a local radio show. Immediately following, his mother - my beloved grandmother Maria Emelia - suffered a stroke from which she would never recover and she died in 1991.

The Black Chief was more than just a politician. He was one of the last Uruguayan populist leaders who had emerged from the old Batllismo school of political thinking. . The Batllismo approach to governing was unique among governments in the Americas. It was founded on the work of Jose Pedro Varela in 1868 and later embraced by President José Batlle y Ordóñez.

Batllismo proponents share a deep belief that the conditions for a successful society must include a profound sense of equality and solidarity combining a respect for institutions of the State along with political and individual liberty. Batllismo support has been a cornerstone of the majority political Colorado Party for many years. Within the framework of democracy, they believed it was possible to lay a foundation to integrate political freedoms with a modified welfare state. In that way, they believed they could provide a much quicker solution to the wealth discrepancies found under capitalism.

This approach was why my father loved democracy and was so committed to the Colorado Party. He always considered democracy a miracle. He believed that he was living proof of that miracle. Here was a man who emerged from one of the country's poorest neighborhoods. Yet he was able to reach the highest political positions without ever forgetting where he came from and why he was in power. It was not uncommon to find him sitting in a street with a group of people or in a bar on the square talking with people from all walks of life. He was respected because he was one of them.

For years, my father was a symbol of hope to Uruguay. Their presence was living proof "that democracy is a miracle that we must preserve." He never lost his gift to break down the barriers imposed by social and economic differences to find common ground. Even when his self-imposed exile began in 1971, he was not forgotten.

He was re-elected Senator again soon after his return to Uruguay in 1985. In 1989 he became a Congressman, then Senator again in 1994. He would be remembered as one of Uruguay's premier statesmen whose career spanned more than 40 years - all as a man of the people. My father even held the respect of his opponents. Opposition member Luis Alberto Heber of the National Party praised my father as "a tough opponent but at the same time a great friend with whom one could talk and agree." In 1999 my father even occupied the Presidency of Uruguay for a few days as a temporary replacement to then-President Julio Maria Sanguinetti.

I think my father was never able to fully grasp his own achievements. The glory did not change him, the power did not corrupt him He always characterized humility as the greatest virtue. He had no attachment to money - his first new car came near the end of his life. He loved the people of Uruguay above all. In his heart he always remained the humble child helping others outside the cemetery.

In 1990, my father helped me get a job in the federal bank in Montevideo, very close to the university. Banking paid well at that time in Uruguay. I remember the day before I started working my father picked me up from the bus terminal across from the bank. He told me,

"You need to think of this job as temporary, do not see your future in this job. Study and get a better job, one where you will be able to send your resignation letter to the President of this bank thanking him for the job."

I had also started to get involved in the Colorado Party nd began to spend my evenings at party headquarters. There, along with the other younger members, we would spend long hours imagining ways to fix the problems of the nation and win elections. I already understood the precepts of the Batllismo Movement from my father's books and I was in love with the nation they had started building in the beginning of the 1900's.

I was now 19 years old. I had finally reached an age and level of understanding where the idealism of my father's books made great sense to me. Even after my mother changed my name everyone knew my last name and who my father was in the Colorado Party.

In January 1991, my father's girlfriend called me to encourage me to speak with him about recovering my original last name. She wanted me to use his birthday party on January 15, 1991, to make the announcement. I spoke to my father about my mother had forced the name change and we put a plan together to restore my real identity. Even the prospect of recovering my name was thrilling to me. I forced myself not to get my hopes up.

The date finally arrived when I could address the Court to appeal to get my identity restored. The Court said my case was not reversible. The judicial system of Uruguay ruled against me thus I was unable at that time to recover my real identity. Without it, I felt that I would never be able to truly be myself. Many people, even some family members, said I just wanted to recover my name to use its power and recognition in politics. What they could not understand was that my spirit was bigger than that. I did not care about the influence of the name. I knew I would be able to achieve my goals regardless of what my last name was.

History shows that when people try to leverage their famous last name for unearned advantage, it rarely turns out well – often it even backfires on them. It is up to each of us who want respect to earn it. I learned at an early age that with or without a famous last name, I had the drive to achieve my dreams. Even still, it would have been a great reconcilliation for both me and my father if I had been able to legally share my birth name with my real father once again.

I pressed forward on my journey into maturity and adulthood. There were so many times, so many nights, I was petrified by the unknown and the future. One moment I walked with total confidence. However, there were also times I did not know if I would be able to go through all that would be ahead. Now I listen to people talk about Post-Traumatic Stress Disorder (PTSD) and the list of symptoms seemed all too real to me.

I look back on all the times I was in peril. I rarely felt like I had time to recover from one event before the next one arrived. I remember I was in Montevideo, where I had a good job. I had everything to start a new life, but I often felt I could not function with so much emptiness in my soul. It felt like everybody around me had their own circle, their own world. I was not part of any of them, and I didn't have enough people close to me to make my own world.

As time passed, I learned that the human spirit can adapt and I quickly learned to count on myself. One cold night sitting alone in the middle of a square in Montevideo, I kept thinking about the insistent ideas my mother had put in my mind. The memory of her pleading that if I cut them off, I would never be anybody. I would end up hungry and sleeping in the streets. Even though there were a few times that I had slept in the streets and did go hungry, I always knew that it was only temporary. I also knew that I was somebody and had value. I just did not know yet who I was and how to move forward.

After working in banking for a year, I received an offer to work for a Congressman. The laws allow every Congressman to ask have a federal employee assigned to work for him. My father did not like the idea and told me I should turn it down. However, I fought for the chance and took it against his advice. I learned the hard way that he was correct about this Congressman. Still, I remained actively involved in politics until 1994 when I moved back to Mercedes and tried to organize a new line inside the

Colorado Party. My father did not think much of my idea. He had very strong control within the Colorado Party and he used it to make it impossible for me to promote it. Instead of working it out with him or trying to understand, I got fed up with politics and decided to return to banking. I found myself soon after working at a small branch in the city of Fray Bentos.

By March 1995, I was still working in banking again but I felt morally broken. I was already a heavy smoker and to make things worse, I started drinking. I just let the stream of my life take me anywhere, just doing enough to keep my job. In the meantime, I had just turned 24 and my personal life was going nowhere. I had little to show for it but a string of bad relationships and the belief that nothing was good enough for me. I continued looking for several more years trying to find myself. I needed to discover who I was and why God had placed me here. I continued to look for things that would give my life meaning and allow me to experience the peace. I needed a sense of purpose that still eluded me. It would be some time before I would find answers for the things I sought.

Chapter 11

Democracy Regains A Foothold

Uruguay was changing politically once again. With the return of democracy, most of our people believed the threat of terrorism and Marxism was in the past. Both had been tried-and-failed movements. Under democracy, the future felt much brighter. True, the socialist and communist movements were still weak in Uruguay but the concepts they promoted were still present. Only the tactics of implementation had changed. Even as a political novice, I could see the enemy was still at the gate.

The terrorists from the 1960s and 1970s were now old men and women. They were now emerging once again from the shadows. This time, however, they pretended to make it look like they had matured to become the politicians of the 1990s. As Congressmen and Senators, they used their newfound political influence to push their changes into law instead of relying solely on crime and violence to control the country. How ironic to see them now campaigning on promises to end the social injustice and end the corruption they themselves were known for. All they would accomplish once again would be to replace the current democratic system of civil liberties and freedom with their own, more brutal version. If they succeeded, disrupting capitalism would also certainly be within their power. Socialists never seem to grasp that capitalism, however imperfect, is by far the best way to generate the wealth for a nation that has ever been developed. They always failed to see what Winston Churchill observed in a speech on Nov. 11, 1947:

"Capitalism is the world's worst economic system, except for all the others."

An anti-democracy coalition was formed called the Board Front which soon started to aggressively attract followers. The economy was already in peril before the military relinquished power. In their wake, they left behind a terrible political and economic inheritance for the newly-elected democratic leaders to deal with it. They had been very aggressive in spending to modernize Uruguay's infrastructure and on social programs while in power. The repayment schedule to international banks meant that important revenues needed to grow the country would now be diverted to debt repayment. Budget cuts and austerity would be both inevitable and very unpopular. I now believe some of the best thinkers in the former dictatorship realized what was coming and chose to relinquish power to avoid the unrest that was certain to follow.

Broad Front solidified as the most prominent leftist group. They already had plans in place to use the declining economy as a weapon to agitate the nation. In reality, Broad Front was simply a coalition of communists, anarchists, socialists and Tupamaros. How they ever believed Socialism was an improvement is why I called them the coalition of "No Sense." Discontent would restore them to power but nothing for the people would come of it except loss of liberty and economic oppression. The only Broad Front end-game they would achieve was to be enable a small group of their friends in the high-ranking party faithful to siphon off wealth from government for personal gain while leaving the people to suffer.

Broad Front focused their efforts on infiltrating and influencing two main sectors: education, and unions. They rightly believed having control of these two groups could control the people over the long run. Their coalition received more and more votes in every election until they were the majority party. Success for them meant doom for the economy, for civil liberties, and the country. It was yet another repackaging of the failed message of socialism. Once more, anti-Americanism, renouncing international debt, and promoting class warfare became their mainstream political message. It broke my heart to see that their plan would probably work. They would ultimately accomplish their goal of an eventual socialist takeover in little more than a decade without firing a shot.

Chapter 12

The Mujica Factor

Jose Mujica was born on May 20, 1935. His father was a small farmer who went bankrupt shortly before his death in 1940. At the time, Mujica was 5 years old. Poverty and deprivation heavily influenced his youth and his entire life.

In the early 1960s, Mujica had been involved in creating the newly-formed Tupamaros movement. They were the armed socialist political group inspired and encouraged by the Cuban Revolution. In 1969, he participated in the brief takeover of Pando, a town close to Montevideo. For this act he was later convicted by a military tribunal under the government of Jorge Pacheco Areco.

As an early Tupamaro leader, Mujica proved very resourceful. He was captured, jailed, escaped, and hunted by the military on four different occasions. He was among the political prisoners who escaped from the Punta Carretas Prison in 1971. He was eventually re-captured in 1972 and shot by the police six times. He survived his injuries and was returned to prison after a lengthy stay in the hospital. After the military coup in 1973, Mujica was transferred to a military prison where he served a dozen more years.

By 1985, the constitutional democracy was restored and the military had relinquished political power. Mujica was freed under the Amnesty law which protected terrorists and related military criminals from prosecution in the courts.

By this time, most believed the Tupamaro Marxist ideas had no more place in Uruguayan society. That is, everyone but the Tupamaros. Several years after that, Mujica and the Tupamaros joined with other left-wing organizations to create the Movement of Popular Participation (MPP). Their party was quickly accepted within the Broad Front coalition. As one of the members of Broad Front, Mujica never gave up believing in the message of socialism above all. Now as the Tupamaros emerged from the shadows once again, they were cloaked as just another of the socialist factions within Broad Front.

Broad Front's success in getting candidates in public office grew with each subsequent election. It was in the 1994 general elections that Mujica was finally elected to the National Assembly. He became a Congressman in 1994, then was elected as a Senator in 1999. The MPP continued to grow in popularity and rack up votes, partly due to Mujica's populist appeal with the poor. By 2004, MPP had become the largest faction within the Broad Front coalition.

The 2004 elections saw Mujica once again re-elected to the Senate. This time, the MPP collected over 300,000 votes, thus consolidating its position as the primary political force within Broad Front. In March of 2005, President Tabaré Vázquez appointed Mujica as the Minister of Livestock, Agriculture and Fisheries. This would be his first nationally prominent role in a presidential administration and would become his stepping stone to the presidency.

José Mujica's campaign for the Presidency was finally successful in 2009. He became President of Uruguay on March 1, 2010. When Mujica took office, he was sworn in by Lucia Topolansky, the President of the Senate. Topolansky was also Mujica's partner and wife during their years together as an anarchists. Reaching the highest political offices may have been a dream for them, but for those who loved the Republic and the Democracy, it was a nightmare and a shame.

Topolansky had been one of Mujica's lifelong fellow Tupamaros starting back in the 1970s. Unlike Mujica, she came from a family of privilege. This allowed her to gain a reputation as something of a scholar and accomplished musician before and during her Tupamaro days. She was also ultimately imprisoned for those activities for 13 years under the military regime as was Mujica.

After her release through the Amnesty, she built a successful political career of her own. During her husband's presidential administration, it became necessary to remove Raul Sendic as vice president during a troubling corruption scandal. Sendic, who resigned as VP in 2017, was one Mujica's old cronies from his Tupamaro days. This meant that the President of the Senate would be elevated to the vice presidency. To further the irony and insult to the nation, Lucia Topolansky was sworn in as Vice President in 2017. Thus, the husband-and-wife team of former Tupamaros were free to finish their terms as President and Vice President.

During the transition to socialism, the labor unions became nothing more than another arm of the socialist party. As they grew stronger, they also became more aggressive at retaliating against members who disagreed. An example happened to me in 2000 when I was questioned by the President of the Banking Union about my lack of participation in the strike. I told him I would not strike against the government because my father was a Senator. The Union President told me they would retaliate against me. I politely responded, "You can go buy some Vaseline and shove your union up your butt".

The unions also controlled the promotion and evaluation committees. As a result, my chance for promotion or receiving a decent job performance assessment was gone. There were thousands of people who did not join the strikes yet received no retaliation from the unions. However, I was one of the few people that the Banking Union actually expelled. I always marveled why people accepted all these new social justice principles when they came at such a high price.

For this reason. unions were able to hold the government hostage as they had essentially become an extension of a leftist power movement. "Paralyze" was a term the unions liked to use. The banking unions were the most powerful among them. They could bring the financial system of the country to a halt for weeks and often months. The education unions also staged strikes, causing a decline in the both the number of students and the quality of their education. Public transportation unions were also very powerful, especially in the big cities where mass transportation was widely used.

Federal, state and private unions in Uruguay are protected if they take over public and private property and deem the action as an "occupation". Even students were seen taking over middle schools, high schools and universities could and did do this. Occupation is a Marxist tactic that somehow became protected by law.

I asked myself how Uruguay could attract foreign investments with all of this going on? Who would want to come and invest in a country filled with regulations, and high taxes where businesses are already unable to provide a steady flow of work? What sane company would build a factory in a country where unions and workers could take control by simply declaring their actions an Occupation?

Union activists and leaders became the new patrons of the working class, destroying the free marketplace in their wake. The list of nations that allow the government and unions to confiscate private property through the rule of law all quickly become failed states. The list is topped by "socialist paradise" countries like Cuba and Venezuela that are now horrible places to live because of this reality. For example, when someone leaves Cuba for the United States the Cuban government seizes their private property. In the case of Venezuela, if your private property survives being looted it is quickly nationalized.

The constant aggression from unions made it almost impossible for workers to keep a job without joining the union. The corruption of the goals and the leadership and had transformed them into something other than a collective worker's union - they now looked and acted like a kind of organized crime syndicate. They used intimidation and even veiled threats of violence to push the ideals of the more radical left groups in Uruguay. The unions no longer respected the voice of their members. They operated like their own unaccountable power structures. If they called for a protest or strike, the members who did not participate paid a heavy price in the form of retaliation. To make things worse, union officials demanded increased roles within all of the Federal power structures. Their demands included, for example, a seat on the evaluation and promotion committees. It was just another example of the way Socialism fosters a terrible and oppressive system. My challenge - my mission - remains calling out such corruption for what it is so those who are affected by it can make better decisions while they still can about who they choose to represent them.

I chose to call this chapter The Mujica Factor for a reason. The story of Jose Mujica and his wife, Lucia Topolansky, is a powerful example. It shows what happens when a country makes the worst possible choices of who should lead their nation. I understand it when people become impatient with the speed at which reforms are made in a democracy. However, that is never a good reason to make bad choices at the ballot box. Ironically, those bad choices ultimately lead to repressive regimes like Broad Front. Socialism is a political wolf in sheep's clothing. It promises prosperity but its reality is consistently destroying financial incentive and economic development everywhere it is tried. In the end it actually ends up stopping or preventing the very reforms the people desired in the first place.

After 15 years of majority socialist rule, Uruguay has little to show for it except an even more enormous public debt and economic stagnation. Societal despair is also at an all-time high due to record rates of crime, including murder. There is a morbid joke that the only businesses doing well are the ones installing security systems and bars on windows. These are the things that always seem to arrive immediately after majority socialist rule begins. Now, in 2022, Uruguay looks poised to once again choose a conservative democratic government. Let's hope they govern well before people forget and choose socialism once again.

Chapter 13

Fading

In 2001, I found the angel who is now my wife. She is heavily vested in patience and in whose big heart I we have been able to share as we build our lives. In 2002 we were eating together and she told me she thought the country was going to hell. Then, she looked straight at me and said,
"I think we should leave and start over somewhere else."

I could not believe what I was hearing! I stood up and threw my dinner plate as I stormed out of the room. How could I leave my country? The thought was very troubling to me. I tried to get some perspective. I realized I needed to speak with my father.

I tried to make arrangements only to learn that my father had become very ill. He had married one of his assistants some time ago and when he became ill, she isolated him away from everybody. I was aware of this but always felt that my father was an adult and if one day he wanted to reach out to some of us, he would reach. That was also my message to anyone who asked.

About the same time, I was sitting in a bus terminal in Mercedes when an old friend sat down beside me. While we waited for the bus, we start talking. He said he had been in the capitol just the week before and he had visited my father in the hospital. I was surprised and saddened as he described how sick and lonely my father was. I immediately decided to go and visit him as soon as possible.

When I arrived, I was told that his wife had given orders that no one was allowed to visit him. But as you can probably guess, nothing could stop me. I traveled to Montevideo to see him in March, 2003 and I could not believe his condition. During one of his surgeries months before, they had removed his vocal cords and were now feeding him through a stomach tube. He was happy but nervous to see me, telling me that his wife must not find me there. He gave me the times to visit when she would not be around.

My father was always a heavy smoker. Never less than 2 packs a day for most of his life. No surprise when he developed both throat cancer and emphysema. Years ago, when I was assisting in his political meetings, he was always running out of cigarettes. His gaze would find me across the room and with his eyes he would tell me to go buy more cigarettes for him. Those cigarettes and good wines were his companions for many years. How strange it was to see such a passionate and strong orator like him without his favorite tool - his voice.

As his illness advanced, the efforts of his wife to isolate him had greatly upset me. However, I said nothing to avoid bringing more suffering into my father's life. Instead, I went to the hospital one day, hoping to confront her outside. I found out she was coming from Mercedes on a bus, so I went to the terminal to wait for her. It was well after midnight and I was standing in front of a glass door with an elevator on my left. She walked into the terminal and went to the other side of the elevator. It took me some time to push through the large crowd of people that were there. As I reached the other side, I saw a man hugging her and they immediately left together. She never saw me. Through some relatives, I found out the "mystery man" was in fact one of my father's doctors. I later also found out that word of my discovery had reached the owner of the hospital. I learned on my return that he was no longer employed there.

I always why the doctors and nurses who attended my father always seemed very nervous. Someone very close to my father quietly told me that his wife had already begun disposing of my father's entire wardrobe. Most of his things from their home were already gone. It is one thing to realize that a loved one is probably not coming home from the hospital. Many people and his family had been hoping and praying for his recovery. The nagging question, for which I still have not found an answer was why she seemed so absolutely certain he wasn't returning home. The unease of the medical staff when she was around had always seemed suspicious as well. I never confronted her but I determined not to let her seeming betrayal of my father go unchallenged. Sometime after his death, I drew public attention to their situation by publishing an article about the events I witnessed as the beloved Black Chief fought his illness. I left nothing out, including my discovery in the bus station. I later learned she was very angry with me. So be it.

A few weeks later I was in Argentina when I received the call saying my father was getting worse and I needed to return to Uruguay right away. He was already in a coma when I entered his hospital room. I will be honest and tell you that my first reaction was to turn around and leave. It broke my heart to see him in that condition. I asked the nurse to leave me alone with him; she told me that she could not do so because hospital orders required her to stay. Everybody else left the room, and the nurse moved to a corner. I felt as if I could barely stand. I do not know who or how, but as I stood in that room someone was holding me up by my shoulders. I looked around and there was only me and the nurse, several feet away. I always wondered about that presence.

I spoke to my father, still unconscious,

"I cannot believe you will leave mad at me."

When I asked him for his forgiveness, his eyes filled up with tears. Even in his coma it was clear he could hear me. I knew in my heart that it was his time. I thought it would be a good idea to help him be ready to go. I reminded him of the good friends that were waiting for him along with his family. Surely, he would finally see his brother and sister again and most importantly, his father who died when he was very young. Surely, he would also see his mother, my beloved Grandma Maria Emelia, who died after the stroke caused by the slurs of that radio show. I told him we would be okay here until we are together again so he was free to go, go.

I took a shower, put on my best suit and prepared to wait as long as necessary. He fought for another 20 hours until finally, he passed into eternity on July 31, 2003, at the age of 70.

The funeral followed in Montevideo. It was filled with family, friends, and all of his political allies and opponents.

Everyone who had supported him and those he had supported throughout his political life were there. Flower shops for miles surrounding Montevideo all ran out of red carnations, the symbol of the Colorado Party. The next morning, we traveled with his body to Mercedes, the place of his birth. He would rest forever in the same cemetery that he knew like the palm of his hand because he had spent so much time there as a kid. I remember seeing a middle-aged man crying as he asked me, "What do we do now, without him?" I could see in his eyes the pain and despair.

Several elected officials from the traditional parties gave speeches honoring him because he was a beloved statesman, friend of the common man, and had even been President for a short time. The government paid him many special honors. I can still hear the volleys of the Honor Guard's rifle squad. I remember the planes flying low overhead and the sound of the military band. I did not help carry his coffin. Instead, I walked behind with his people. Inside the cemetery, I kept my distance and rested my tired body against a wall. A hundred feet away, the last minutes of my father's funeral were wrapping up.

A Senator made a statement I will not forget,

> *"This little town let the whole country have the service of this patriot, and now we bring him back to you, to his people, to his town."*

The loud applause filled the quiet cemetery. The thousands of people there cried out in a chorus of voices. Over the loudspeaker someone declared, "Yes, he is back and with clean hands." This was the most important treasure I would ever receive from him. I felt that day that my heritage had been miraculously restored. Now I was free – to stay or to leave. While I was walking away, one veteran activist of the Colorado Party called out to me in a loud voice,

"Now, now is your time."

I turned around and looked straight at him with a sad smile and replied without pausing to think,

"No, it is not. I'm leaving."

I had come full circle somehow. Not long ago, at the mere suggestion of leaving our country, I had flown into a rage. But my reaction had caused me to think. I eventually realized my anger was so extreme because I knew she was right!

Once I started looking around, there was a reality that I could finally see but not accept until now. Today, it became clear that my father's death was not just a personal loss. The grief on the faces of those we encountered showed me that my father's life had also represented hope. Because of men like him, the heart and soul of our country still believed in the principles of a just democratic rule. As long as there still were men like him, it felt like there was still hope. That hope was fading fast, and for that reason I knew she was right…it was time to start over in America – the best example of democracy the world has ever known.

Chapter 14

A New Land

> *"I've always believed that this blessed land was set apart in a special way, that some divine plan placed this great continent here between the oceans to be found by people from every corner of the Earth who had a special love for freedom and the courage to uproot themselves, leave homeland and friends, to come to a strange land. And coming here they created something new in all the history of mankind–a land where man is not beholden to government, government is beholden to man."*
> - Ronald Reagan

My life was starting over, on another continent with another climate and another culture. I was opening my eyes to this new land called America, the land of opportunities. I knew I was an outsider just coming in. South America, the land I called home was gone, at least for me. It had become only a piece of land. It was a land where many people lived who still I missed and, of course, a big trunk of memories.

I arrived in 2003 with the woman I loved who would soon become my wife. From the first time we thought about living in America, the main goal was to become a part of this society. Our first step was to work hard so we could master the language. We needed to be able to listen and learn from others. We needed to be able to communicate with those around us.

Second, we needed to understand and respect the laws of this new land and to honor our new home, live under the same laws, and to earn the chance to live with the same liberty. But it was not easy here. Old fears of the past and the absence of so many familiar comforts was unsettling. In my mind, the country of which my father dreamed was still alive. I envisioned people fighting for his shared dreams even though I knew that dream had faded. It somehow made it even more difficult to be here.

In my new land I started asking myself question after question. What was this country about? Why was this land blessed with so much prosperity? It was founded at relatively the same time as the most of other countries in the Americas; it has many of the same natural resources and shares the same oceans. What made the difference? Why was this America so prosperous?

I enjoyed blending into the social order. I worked to earn the respect of my neighbors, even when some looked at me strangely. Often, I longed to go back and start over, but the Uruguay I knew was gone. I would find the same houses on the same streets and with many of the people I knew still living in the same neighborhoods. But "my country" wasn't there. Eventually I understood that a nation is not just land with rules, infrastructure and people, it was more than that...a nation is a place with a heart and a spirit. And that spirit back home had continued to die a little more each time someone like my father passed away.

After all I had gone through and all I have described, waves of doubt still often swept over me that a new life here would be impossible. Our youngest daughter was still a newborn, so I had to find the strength to keep going. We were three souls bound as a family trying to make our way in a huge new country. It is said that every journey begins with a single step. For us, every day was one step, then another, then another.

I knew it was time to tackle one of my main challenges - my addiction to tobacco. My daily dose was 2-3 packs of cigarettes a day. I knew I must give priority to this issue because without my health, I would not be able to achieve anything else. I dreaded the vision of my daughter standing on the side of my bed as I died because I wasn't strong enough to fight this addiction. The image of my father's death still haunted me.

I'm not going to say it was easy; I tried and failed numerous times until I finally was able to quit smoking - for good. This wasn't being a quitter. When someone quits, it usually means they give up trying. To quit smoking – that requires someone to be a fighter. I never gave up even through the failures. I had to remind myself I would win this fight. Finally, I quit smoking!

I started running to help my lungs recover and it became a healing process for my mind as well. I used my time running to fight my internal struggles, to strengthen my soul. I needed to find the motivation every day. After several years of running, I grew stronger and began competing in running events. Eventually I ended up finishing five full 26.2-mile marathons! The sense of accomplishment was great but long distances had started to feel boring. Soon, I discovered something even better. It was an event that combined swimming, biking, and running together – The Ironman.

I added swimming and biking to my training routine and soon I was hooked! I began training hard to compete in the Ironman 70.3 Series. This felt like just the challenge I needed. The Ironman 70.3 is an extreme challenge to both your mental and physical strength. It requires you to swim

1.2 miles, bike for 56 miles, then immediately run a half-marathon for 13.1 miles – 70.3 miles in all. I trained and competed in three Ironman events and completed them all!

Running and the triathlon discipline gave me the skills I had been missing: patience, perseverance, physical stamina, mental strength. Those many hours to myself helped to restore order to my mind.

We arrived in America with almost nothing and we initially had to rely on the kindness of people we encountered and some government assistance to survive. I appreciated the help because I knew it was temporary until we were able to work, earn our way, and live independently.

People would tell me if I went to a certain place, I could get free furniture there. Then I could go to an office where I could get a check to buy food. Then this place would provide me with free clothing and at that place I could get some free food. Free, free, free stuff! I did not like it! I just needed some work.

I was not afraid to begin from zero because I knew my potential. I wanted a situation where I could develop myself; see what I was capable of achieving – without the handouts. I did not want my greatest skill to be how to acquire free benefits.

The first skills I used after arriving were the skills I brought with me: To be flexible to learn, flexible to develop, able to grow, to be willing to work hard. I also understood from day one that I needed to submit myself to the same laws that the American people lived by each day. What better way to prove to them I wanted to be a part of them than by honoring their rules?

Even still, there were difficulties adapting I had not anticipated. Several people kept telling me I would get nowhere because I wasn't white, and too bad that I wasn't black enough either. I learned that being Latino was its own kind of obstacle in America. It did not take long for me to begin placing blame for everything that went wrong in my life on my race. It was faulty thinking and it caused me to make mistakes. What better way to avoid responsibility for yourself than to blame somebody else?

I'm not going to deny there are bad people in America who want to abuse others. Those people exist in every country. I recognize that it is not a perfect world. It took time to realize I was letting those imperfections and bad actors blind me to what was really behind my newly adopted nation - a people with strong heart and a spirit that stood for achievement!

I was intrigued that a country so full of opportunities to work and achieve had so many people who instead settled for chasing and claiming government benefits they had not earned or didn't need. There is a time and place for such programs but it was the abuse of the system that I hated. I was determined to not be that kind of person.

Friendships and relationships are built through processes of support and trust over time. I didn't expect anyone to accept me as a part of them until I had proven myself to them. I always tried to put myself in their shoes. What would I do if someone came to me yelling, making demands, and not respecting the rules? Such behavior certainly undermines any willingness in the other person to help. I forced myself to battle between the independence that I learned the hard way and the need for connection and meaningful relationships. A balance in both things is a necessity in almost every culture. I worked hard and learned needed skills. Every step was difficult, but I did better every day. All the while, I continued monitoring the situation in Uruguay.

My father's death had affected me in more ways than I expected and certainly more ways than I was willing to admit. It wasn't easy to deal with it while I was working on so many other issues. A letter I wrote here was published in a newspaper back in Uruguay. It was an honest and accurate expression of those feelings.

> *To my father,*
> *It has been many days that I have been away from our land. I am getting used to the distance, but I cannot forget you and I decided to write and share this with your people, with those who loved you so much.*
> *Surely you ask if you are missed, if we feel your absence, if we feel the absent breath. How could I walk your streets without feeling you? How do I breathe that air that you breathed and you made so distinct?*
> *You are missed and life has become agitated and nervous without you, as if we had been defeated.*
> *For me you will always be there, with your head held high and your hand cutting the wind of liberty that imprinted you in so many lives. This same liberty allows me to walk alone and away today.*
> *Even confronting the illness, the malice, the slander, the indecent conduct, the threat of such gratuitous cruelty that infringes upon us, that indignant and evil being, I continue being free to keep you alive through these printed words, this never overcame me.*
> *But do not think that I'm so sad that I do not smile when I remember you. I can say I am at peace with you and with me. I will never forget the evil, its face or its name, and sooner or later I will return to unravel the many doubts that have stayed with me lately. I think the truth is much*

darker than the facts that I know have been revealed.

I was happy to spend those last days with you because we had missed so much time with each other, although I was terrified to say goodbye to you. When we returned to Mercedes and I saw all the people there, I understood that you were with them and always would be just as you are with me today in my sleepless nights, in my far away and nostalgic evenings.

I sometimes think how empty my life would have been without your presence, if we had not had that time together. I recognize the differences we had, ridiculous disagreements between two generations that were trying to know each other. If I could live my life again, I would seek another path between us and I know you would as well.

But at the end, life did us justice and we were together physically those last days, in the spiritual. A farewell will never be necessary because you are in my heart and always will be. Thus, my dear old man, I will see you soon, I will see you later, because sooner or later we will find each other again. You should rest assured that I didn't carry your absence all the way here, because you are in my children, in my dreams, and in my horizons, and as such you will never just be part of my past, but my present and my future.

And it is, my learned old man, this other Labrador that you raised, both servant and rebellious, sometimes gentle and always vigilant, that today licks his wounds in the darkness. As a popular dog, he will wander on your narrow paths and live in Uncle Justo's bloody songs, until he too dies, one lonely and rabid day, from his

innocent fondness or of some violent love, but of love no doubt.
Your son,
Luis

I returned to Uruguay in 2004 to attend the first anniversary of my father's death. I didn't find him in the cemetery or in the ceremonies; he was gone and the nation I knew growing up was leaving us too.

In 2004, the left-wing coalition won the national elections. Their plan to disrupt the system had finally triumphed after forty years. They had once tried to bring about this change with weapons, murders, kidnappings, and theft. But nothing worked as well as when they put down their AK47's and picked up the vote to achieve the change they pursued. On the other hand, the traditionalist party did not adapt to the changing tactics; they did not develop fresh new leaders and squandered their opportunity. Instead they tried to mimic the popular ideas of leftist groups and moved to the left, abandoning many of their core principles.

They also failed to implement educational programs for their citizens teach them the concepts they needed to secure their liberties. The leftists were now hiding their crimes under a romantic veil. They were somehow no longer domestic terrorists anymore! Instead, they had re-cast themselves as Robin Hood-type heroes. They used their community programs to teach their own doctrine to the citizens. They would use the schools, the media, and their neighborhood programs. The traditionalist democratic parties were responsible for their own undoing. They remained lost in their own chaos and their own ridiculous internal fights while the cancer of socialism continued to spread - it finally killed them.

The entire political strategy of the left before and while in power was based upon lies. All their promised reforms were rhetoric without tangible results. They promised to finish off Capitalism and Imperialism. They promised to stop payment of the international debt. They promised new opportunities to the people. They promised Hope and Change. What they actually delivered was more welfare, more free things to entice the people into believing that a better comfort level was just around the corner.

Their economic policies were also a disaster. A main export of Uruguay is beef, but yet the people were forced to pay impossibly high prices for it. Insecurity was everywhere, with people feeling the need to make their homes into jails with bars in the windows for their own protection. Drug abuse increased. They are still paying the international debt. They failed to bring their revolution to Uruguay.

I'm still looking at the history of Uruguay in disbelief. The socialists kidnapped, robbed and killed in the name of social justice and socialism. After 40 years, they won the elections and so far, have done almost nothing even after several presidential terms. They did increased taxes, of course.

As a result, Uruguay has become a shadow, a sham, with a president who acts and looks more like the penguin in a Batman movie than a national leader. He remains an amnestied domestic terrorist, who calls himself the poorest president of the world. I would ask - where are all the miraculous results they promised and failed to deliver? Some have even been suggested that Mujica be nominated for a Nobel peace prize. I would simply ask – for what? Instead, he seems much more comfortable in his role as a terrible actor in a bad movie than President of a Republic.

Chapter 15

The Parallels

*"History doesn't repeat itself, but it often rhymes." –
Mark Twain*

After a few years in America, I started to see signs that the same things I lived through in Uruguay were happening in the U.S. The first time it occurred to me, I thought I was paranoid. However, the patterns kept revealing themselves and I realized a shift was underway.

I had not studied much of the history of America from the 1960's to the early 2000's until after I arrived here in 2003. Once I did, I was shocked at how many similarities I could see between both nations over the last forty years.

Uruguay is a tiny country of only 3.5 million people in southern South America. It is slightly more than half the size of Arizona. Like the U.S., it has ample coastline and shares land borders with only 2 other countries – Argentina to the west and Brazil to the northeast. Mostly, this is where the physical similarities between the two countries ends. America, by contrast, is a giant land in every way with a population of over 330 million. That is why I was amazed when I began to compare what I seeing in America with the history of the country of my birth. It appeared to me that the difference in size does not matter.

I mentioned previously that I came to the United States because America was so widely admired as a great capitalist nation and a land of opportunity. It is possibly the greatest example of prosperity, freedom and liberty in history. That is why I was horrified that America appeared to be embracing the same socialist doctrines and principles which brought the toxic effects of Marxism to Uruguay and, ultimately, the majority of South and Central America.

Many of the changes of the last 40 years in Uruguay were implemented by people who had been the hard-core Marxists and terrorists in the 1970s and 1980s. Many of them had actually been jailed for violent crimes like murder and bank robbery they had committed in the furtherance of their cause.

In an earlier chapter, I described the events in March 1985, when the military dictatorship finally returned power to the newly-elected democratic government. In those early days the public conversation all centered around the great collective relief that democratic change had finally come. National sentiment included a strong push for reconciliation to help heal the nation. The new democratic majority addressed this by passing several laws granting broad Amnesty for both former Tupamaros for crimes of terror, and military officers who had grossly overstepped their limits suppressing dissent.

Much began to change soon after the Marxists were released from prison in 1985. Amnesty meant that those who had been jailed were once again free to push for the changes they still wanted in the way the country was ruled. However, they exchanged their guns and clubs for the popular vote. They worked to use the ballot box get elected to seats of power. Their efforts took several years but finally began to succeed. During the mid-1990s they began a serious push to replace democratic reform with majority socialist rule.

Let me review some of the changes brought by those socialists once Amnesty set the stage for Uruguay to swing socialist. This list also includes many of the consequences I have witnessed in the name of their social justice. See if any of these changes sound familiar. Also note whether the "solutions" brought the promised results.

Education

Federalized education was one of the main entry points for the radical left. They to begin reforming all subjects in a bid to introduce the kids to socialism as an acceptable mainstream idea. The Teachers' Union, lead by radical leftists, even began to change the way courses were taught in all subjects to indoctrinate kids with leftist ideas of equality. This brought a rapid decline in the quality of public education in Uruguay.

Next. teacher strikes frequently left kids in the streets because both parents needed to work in the difficult economic times. The education strikes began taking a toll on the country and distrust of the government grew for turning a blind eye to the concerns of parents and instead supporting the unions. Parents believed the government in its current democratic form had clear obligations and it was failing their children. The middle class, who could afford private schools, withdrew from the public school system which further undermined the next generations.

As recently as the 1980's, Uruguay was considered a country with a high level of education in Latin America. But by 2011, the educational system had become one of the lowest ranked in Latin America. In 2011, only 42% of Uruguay citizens 20 - 24 years old had any secondary education or technical training compared to the other countries of Latin America - Chile, 82%; Colombia, 65.6%; Peru, 80%, and Panama, 59%.

Firearms

Uruguay has always had strict gun regulations. Even so, those regulations did not stop domestic terrorists from importing all the guns they needed from foreign countries. It also did not prevent these criminals from buying guns on the black market or from stealing them from legal gun shops, even though both activities were illegal as well. Gun laws that are not backed up by effective enforcement are a travesty. Terrorists and criminals ignore these laws completely. Such laws only served to disarm law-abiding citizens, thus preventing them from defending themselves.

However, in 2013, Uruguayan President Mujica (a former terrorist and criminal himself) decided to push ahead and implement even more restrictive gun control regulations. Headlines read: *GOOD NEWS FOR THE OFFENDERS - Only criminals will now be armed.*

Uruguayan President Mujica was himself rumored to have participated in several armed bank robberies. He "left the profession" due to his imprisonment and his age, but still maintained contact with a guild of criminals. One of his closest co-conspirators from the 1960s was Raul Sendic.

Sendic became Mujica's vice-president, but was driven from office in 2017, because of a widespread financial corruption scandal and was ultimately forced to resign. Apparently, still a thief, just not using guns any more.

Crime and Lawlessness

Urban crime and public insecurity in Uruguay have become the top social problems in recent years. Combine the decline in the quality of education with fewer economic opportunities in the smallest country in South America and you have a recipe for an increase in crime. Over the last decade, homicides, thefts, and personal assaults during robberies have been skyrocketing, committed by younger and younger citizens.

Due to increased crime, Uruguayan prisons are filled with these younger offenders. The long-term societal impact will be higher costs to the penal system, more repeat offenders, and greater negative economic impact on citizens. The downward spiral shows no signs of changing until economic development and criminal justice reform takes place.

As mentioned previously, law-abiding citizens now have no legal means to own a firearm and protect themselves and their property from criminals who do not obey gun control laws in any form.

Illegal Drugs

In response to increases in drug trafficking, President Mujica proposed allowing the cultivation, distribution and trade of marijuana under federal regulation. In August, 2013 the Uruguayan House adopted a bill to do so that was eventually passed into law. Passing this legislation established Uruguay as the first nation in the world to legalize the cultivation and sale of marijuana.

Government legalization of production, processing, distribution, and use of marijuana or any addictive substance is a white flag of surrender. The socialist government may have the legal authority to permit drug trafficking in use but they certainly cannot claim the moral authority to do so. No number of laws will regulate man's moral decisions; the education of the people is what will encourage good judgment on issues such as drug use.

There have been alarming changes in the drug trade that have appeared on several fronts. The Chinese government through the Mexican cartels, have been extending their reach into all corners of South America. Fentanyl and meth have become widespread problems in Uruguay just like they have in the rest of the world. A good example of this was the 2021 bust of the largest shipment of methamphetamines ever seen in Latin America.

More and Higher Taxes

Governments addicted to socialism are also addicted to the march of raising taxes. Decades before gaining power, the Broad Front coalition campaigned on a new tax system. Their proposal was a system where the rich pay a confiscatory amount of taxes, described by Broad Front as their "fair share" to help the poor. This approach always looks good on paper but almost never works in practice, especially in a wealthy country like the U.S. Confiscating every dime from every millionaire and redistributing it to the poor would make very little impact. That's because the rich also have little trouble either moving their money or themselves somewhere else. They called it social justice, but I call it tax injustice in Uruguay. Besides, relocating out of the country where they are targeted is easier for the rich than for any of us.

Once the Broad Front coalition gained power, the tax increases on salaries began, with middle class workers carrying the heaviest tax burden while receiving the least benefits from the government. The elites in government escaped their tax burden through loopholes and the extreme poor are unable to contribute. The result is that a once-thriving middle class in the 'Switzerland of South American' has been in decline for over a decade due to over-burdening taxation. All of this comes in the name of social justice, wealth redistribution, or any other label you feel comfortable applying.

The middle class have now become much maligned by the political system "populists." Yet they are the ones that support a large percentage of the economic engine any country. The middle class is reviled and hated by the Broad Front coalition even though they are the ones who spend the most money on goods and services.

Today there are first-class citizens (those who govern, business owners, and their friends), second-class citizens (the nearly non-existent middle class), and the third-class citizens (more than 500,000 workers with wages lower than $450 a month). These are the people who remain captives to the plan of "equity". This type of government dependency is a classic goal and result of socialism.

More Welfare
In 2009, the leftist government created new regulations, including a new institution called Mides. This plan was called and equality plan and was created to give all non-working citizens a salary and a credit card – for not working. I personally interviewed people to see the effects of the new welfare program. I was told by many that I spoke with that they were choosing instead to receive the new benefit.

"Why would I work 8 hours a day, have a schedule, exhaust myself if I can stay home and still get paid?"

Does this sound familiar? That is the sound of history rhyming. Many are now working a side job being paid in cash while remaining on the new welfare plan. The great achievement of the Mides has been the creation of a false economic comfort zone financed on the backs of taxpayers. It has become a tool for the current administration to secure votes from non-working citizens, now happy to enjoy the cushion of this new form of "social justice." In the meantime, the middle class and the senior citizens pay for it in the form of higher taxes and reduced pension benefits.

Immigration

Immigration is without doubt a game-changing event in any society. Although the influence of waves of immigration on nations may not be seen immediately, it can be definitely harmful in the longer term. In the first half of the 1900's, Uruguay received thousands of Communist anarchists escaping Europe. It was these Bolsheviks and Communists that played an important role in the introduction of socialism to a previously democratic Uruguay.

Uruguay has always struggled to grow its population and economy. In the years around WWI, there were very liberal immigration qualification requirements. For years, undesirables, especially from Europe, found a home in

Uruguay. The population grew but not the economy. Unfortunately, one thing the new arrivals were good at was organizing the minority against the silent majority.

As can be seen from this list, sometime we fall prey to the limitations we create and place upon ourselves while trying to do the right thing. Just before the 2008 American presidential elections, an American lawyer who was living in a Chicago mansion, felt compelled to expressed her feelings about this. She had grown up in a simple working-class family. She was able to attend some of the most renowned colleges. After passing the bar, she immediately began work at one of the top law firms in the U.S.

Yet, this lawyer believes America had still not given her enough opportunity. She said,

"... further integration and/or assimilation into a white cultural and social structure that will only allow me to remain on the periphery of society; never becoming a full participant."

That lawyer was Michelle Obama whose husband, Barack Obama, was about to be elected America's next president

In South America, there is a similar history of opponents of democracy claiming they were denied the needed access to educational, economic, and social opportunities. Yet somehow, one young son of Uruguay was able to rise above his childhood poverty. After starting out bringing water and flowers to cemetery patrons for tips he was one day to also become President of the Republic. No complaints from him – just hard work and love of the people.

Chapter 16

The America List

There are insights to be gained by revisiting Uruguay's past and watching it's decline into socialist rule. One of those insights is seeing the way socialism first captured a foothold in Uruguay and comparing that to how the same thing is well underway in the U.S.

There are also similarities in how the Uruguayan Tupamaros went about extending their influence by using violence to force a strong and powerful response from the government. The details of those crimes and acts of terror found in Chapter 5 List of Shame may be unique to Uruguay, but what those acts represents is not.

In America, the Weather Underground played much the same role as did the Tupamaros in Uruguay. Both movements were heavily influenced by Che Guevara during their 'formative years'. No surprise that the Weather Underground has been either linked to, claimed responsibility for, or been convicted of a strikingly similar list of actions and crimes. The Tupamaro list is presented in Chapter 5 as Uruguay's List of Shame.. The American counterpart is presented in this chapter, courtesy of the Weather Underground. Once again, the details come mostly from online wiki-type compilations that have been checked for accuracy against several additional sources and found to be credible.

1969
June 18-22, 1969 – Students for a Democratic Society (SDS) - The SDS National Convention held in Chicago, Illinois. Publication of the founding statement of Weathermen. Members seize control of SDS National Office.

July 1969 – Weatherman members Bernardine Dohrn, Eleanor Raskin, Dianne Donghi, Peter Clapp, David Millstone and Diana Oughton travel to Cuba and meet representatives of the North Vietnamese and Cuban governments.

August 1969 – Weatherman member Linda Sue Evans travels to North Vietnam. Weatherman activists meet in Cleveland, Ohio in preparation for "Days of Rage" protests scheduled for October, 1969 in Chicago.

September 3, 1969 – Female members participate in a "jailbreak" at South Hills High School in Pittsburgh, Pennsylvania where they run through the school shouting anti-war slogans and distributing literature promoting the "National Action." The term "Pittsburgh 26" refers to the 26 women arrested in connection with this incident.

September 24, 1969 – A group of members confront Chicago police during a demonstration supporting the "National Action," and protesting the commencement of the Chicago Eight trial stemming from the 1968 Democratic National Convention.

October 5, 1969 – The Haymarket Police Statue in Chicago is bombed; Weathermen later claim credit for the bombing in their book, Prairie Fire.

October 8-11, 1969 – The "Days of Rage" riots occur in Chicago, damaging a large amount of property. 287 Weatherman members are arrested, some become fugitives when they fail to appear for trial.

November 8, 1969 - Sniper attack on Cambridge police station. Two shots were fired. Two Weathermen, James Kilpatrick and James Reaves, were indicted and subsequently released when a witness recanted his testimony.

November-December 1969 – Karen Ashley and Phoebe Hirsch were among the few Weatherman members to join the first contingent of the Venceremos Brigade (VB) that departs for Cuba to harvest sugar cane.

December 6, 1969 – Bombing of several Chicago police cars parked in a precinct parking lot at 3600 North Halsted Street, Chicago. The WU claims responsibility in Prairie Fire, stating it is a protest of the fatal police shooting of Illinois Black Panther party leaders Fred Hampton and Mark Clark on December 4, 1969.

December 27-30, 1969 – Weathermen hold a War Council in Flint, Michigan, where plans are finalized to change into an underground organization that will commit strategic acts of sabotage against the government. Thereafter they are called Weather Underground Organization.

1970

January, 1970 - Silas and Judith Bissell placed a homemade bomb under the steps of the R.O.T.C. building at the University of Washington. The bomb was made from an electric blasting cap, an alarm clock, a battery, and a plastic bag filled with gasoline and explosives.

February, 1970 – The WU closes the SDS National Office in Chicago, concluding the major campus-based organization of the 1960s. The first contingent of the VB returns from Cuba and the second contingent depart. By mid-February, the bulk of the leading WU members go underground.

February 16, 1970 - A bomb is detonated at the Golden Gate Park branch of the San Francisco police department, killing one officer and injuring a number of other policemen (one seriously). No organization claims credit for either bombing.

February 21, 1970 - the house of Judge Murtagh, who presides over the Panther 21 trial, is fire-bombed by a WU cell in New York City. The same night, Molotov cocktails were thrown at a police car in Manhattan and two military recruiting stations in Brooklyn.

March, 1970 – Warrants are issued for several WU members, who become federal fugitives when they fail to appear for trial in Chicago.

March 6, 1970 – WU members Theodore Gold, Diana Oughton and Terry Robbins are killed in a Greenwich

Village townhouse explosion when a nail-bomb they were constructing detonates. The bomb was intended to be planted at a non-commissioned officer's dance at Fort Dix, New Jersey.

March 30, 1970 – Chicago police discover a WU "bomb factory" on Chicago's north side.

April 1, 1970 - Based on a tip, Chicago police find 59 sticks of dynamite, ammunition, and nitroglycerine in an apartment traced to WU members. The discovery of the WU weapons cache ends WU activity in this city.

April 2, 1970 - A federal grand jury in Chicago returns a number of indictments charging WU members with violation of federal anti-riot laws. A number of additional federal warrants charging "unlawful flight to avoid prosecution" are returned in Chicago based on the failure of WU members to appear for trial in local cases. (The Anti-riot Law charges were later dropped in January, 1974.)

April 15, 1970 – The FBI arrests WU members Linda Sue Evans and Dianne Donghi in New York with the help of WU infiltrator, Larry Grathwohl.

May 10, 1970 – The National Guard Association of the United States building in Washington, D.C. is bombed.

May 21, 1970 – The WU releases its "Declaration of a State of War" communique under Bernardine Dohrn's name.
June 6, 1970 – In a letter, the WU claims credit for bombing the San Francisco Hall of Justice, although no explosion had occurred. Months later, workmen locate an unexploded bomb.

June 9, 1970 - New York City police headquarters is bombed by Jane Alpert and accomplices. Weathermen state this is in response to "police repression". The bomb was made with ten sticks of dynamite. The explosion was preceded by a six-minute warning and subsequently by a WU claim of responsibility.

July 23, 1970 – A federal grand jury in Detroit, Michigan returns indictments against 13 WU members and former WU members charging violations of various explosives and firearms laws (these indictments were later dropped in October, 1973).

July 25, 1970 - The United States Army base at The Presidio in San Francisco is bombed on the 11th anniversary of the Cuban Revolution. On the same day, a branch of the Bank of America is bombed in New York.

July 28, 1970 - Bank of America headquarters in New York City is bombed around 3:50 a.m. WU claims responsibility.

September 15, 1970 – The WU helps Dr. Timothy Leary escape from the California Men's Colony prison.

October 8, 1970 - Bombing of Marin County courthouse. WU states this is in retaliation for the killings of Jonathan Jackson, William Christmas and James McClain.

October 10, 1970 - A Queens traffic court building is bombed. WU claims this is to express support for the New York prison riot.

October 11, 1970 - A courthouse in Long Island City, NY is bombed. An estimated 8 to 10 sticks of dynamite are used. A warning was given around 10 minutes prior to the 1:23 a.m. blast by the WU.

October 14, 1970 - The Harvard Center for International Affairs is bombed by The Proud Eagle Tribe of Weather (later renamed the Women's Brigade of the Weather Underground. WU claims this is to protest the war in Vietnam. The bombing was in reaction to Angela Davis' arrest and was the first action undertaken by an all-women's unit of WU.

October, 1970 - Bernardine Dohrn, Katherine Ann Power, and Susan Edith Saxe were put on the FBI's Ten Most Wanted List.

December, 1970 – Fugitive WU member Caroline Tanker, who fled the country for Cuba, is arrested by the FBI in Pittsburgh, Pennsylvania.

December 5, 1970 - Five Weathermen are captured for trying to bomb First National City Bank of New York and other buildings on the anniversary of the death of Black Panther Fred Hampton. These individuals subsequently plead guilty.

December 11, 1970 - Vivian Bogart and Patricia Mclean from the WU are arrested after throwing an incendiary bomb at the Royal National Bank in NYC around 1:30 a.m.

December 16, 1970 - Fugitive WU member Judith Alice Clark is arrested on the Days of Rage indictments by the FBI in New York.

1971
March 1, 1971 - The United States Capitol is bombed. WU states this is to protest the invasion of Laos. President

Richard M. Nixon denounces the bombing as a "shocking act of violence that will outrage all Americans."

April, 1971 – FBI agents discover what is dubbed "Pine Street Bomb Factory", an abandoned apartment utilized by WU in San Francisco, California.

August 30, 1971 - Bombings of the Office of California Prisons in Sacramento and San Francisco, allegedly in retaliation for the killing of prison inmate George Jackson.

September 17, 1971 - The New York Department of Corrections in Albany, New York is bombed, as per WU to protest the killing of 29 inmates at Attica State Penitentiary.

October 15, 1971 - The bombing of William Bundy's office in the MIT research center.

1972
May 19, 1972 - Bombing of The Pentagon in retaliation for the U.S. bombing raid in Hanoi. The date was chosen for it being Ho Chi Minh's birthday.

1973
May 18, 1973 - The bombing of the 103rd Police Precinct in New York. WU states this is in response to the killing of 10-year-old black youth Clifford Glover by police.

September 19, 1973 – A WU member is arrested by the FBI in New York. Released on bond, this member again submerges into the underground.

September 28, 1973 - ITT headquarters buildings in New York and Rome, Italy are bombed. WU states this is in response to ITT's alleged role in the Chilean coup earlier that month.

Around October, 1973 the Government requested dropping charges against most of the WU members. The requests cited a recent decision by the Supreme Court that barred electronic surveillance without a court order. This decision could hamper prosecution of the WU cases. In addition, the government did not want to reveal foreign intelligence secrets that the court had ordered disclosed.

1974

March 6, 1974 - Bombing of the Department of Health, Education and Welfare offices in San Francisco. WU states this is to protest alleged sterilization of poor women. In the accompanying communiqué, the Women's Brigade argues for the need for women to take control of daycare, healthcare, birth control and other aspects of women's daily lives.

May 31, 1974 - The Office of the California Attorney General is bombed. WU states this is in response to the killing of six members of the Symbionese Liberation Army.

June 17, 1974 - Gulf Oil's Pittsburgh headquarters is bombed. WU states this is to protest the company's actions in Angola, Vietnam, and elsewhere.

July, 1974 – The WU releases the book Prairie Fire, in which they indicate the need for a unified Communist Party. They encourage the creation of study groups to discuss their ideology, and continue to stress the need for violent acts. The book also admits WU responsibility of several actions from previous years. The Prairie Fire Organizing Committee (PFOC) arises from the teachings in this book and is organized by many former WU members.

September 11, 1974 – Bombing of Anaconda Corporation (part of the Rockefeller Corporation). WU states this is in retribution for Anaconda's alleged involvement in the Chilean coup the previous year.

1975

January 29, 1975 - Bombing of the State Department; WU states this is in response to escalation in Vietnam.

January 23, 1975 - Offices of Department of Defense in Oakland are bombed. In a statement released to the press, Weather expressed solidarity with the Vietnamese still fighting against the Thieu regime in Vietnam.

Spring 1975 - WU publishes "Politics in Command," which is its new political-military strategy. It furthers the line of building a legal, above-ground organization and begins to minimize the armed struggle role.

March, 1975 – The WU releases its first edition of a new magazine entitled Osawatomie.

June 16, 1975 - Weathermen bomb a Banco de Ponce (a Puerto Rican bank) in New York; WU states this is in solidarity with striking Puerto Rican cement workers.

July, 1975 - More than a thousand women attend the Socialist Feminist Conference at Antioch College in Yellow Springs, Ohio in which WU supporters attempt to play a major role.

July 11-13, 1975 – The Prairie Fire Organizing Committee (PFOC) holds its first national convention during which time they go through the formality of creating a new organization.

September, 1975 – Bombing of the Kennecott Corporation in Salt Lake City, Utah; WU states this is in retribution for Kennecott's alleged involvement in the Chilean coup two years prior.

1976
1976-1981 - Weather Underground slowly disbands, many members turning themselves in after taking advantage of the Federal Government dropping most charges in 1973 (illegal wiretaps and intelligence sources & methods issues) and of President Jimmy Carter's amnesty for draft dodgers.

1977
February, 1977 - The first issue of Prairie Fire Organizing Committee's magazine, Breakthrough, is published.

Spring, 1977 - The John Brown Book Club compiles articles critical of the old WU leadership and subsequent split in a pamphlet entitled: The Split of the Weather Underground Organization: Struggling against White and Male Supremacy.

November, 1977 - Five WU members are arrested on conspiracy to bomb California State Senator John Brigg's offices. It is later revealed that the Revolutionary Committee and PFOC had been infiltrated, and the arrests were the results of the infiltration. From this point on, some authors argue that the Weather Underground Organization ceases to exist.

1980
July, 1980 - Former WU member, Cathy Wilkerson, surfaces in New York City and is charged with possession of

explosives arising from the 1970 townhouse explosion. She is sentenced to three years in prison.

December 3, 1980 - Bernardine Dohrn and Bill Ayers turn themselves in. Charges against Ayers are dropped in 1973 (illegal wire taps and foreign intelligence sources and methods). Dohrn is placed on probation. It was discovered that the FBI had discussed a plan to kidnap her nephew, among other controversial schemes.

1981
October 20, 1981 - Brinks robbery in which WU members Kathy Boudin, Sam Brown, Judy Clark and David Gilbert and the Black Liberation Army stole over $1.6 million from a Brinks armored car at the Nanuet Mall, near Nyack, New York. The thieves were stopped by police later that day and engaged them in a shootout, killing two police officers and one Brinks guard, as well as wounding several others.

1987
Silas Bissell, a leader of the Weather Underground Organization who was once on the FBI's Ten Most Wanted list, is arrested for bombing ROTC building. His ex-wife, Judith Bissell, served three years for the attempted bombing of CA State Senator John Briggs' office.

The lists of terrorist activities in two democratic Republics thousands of miles apart contains many similarities. If one were to look at other countries fighting a rising tide of socialism, one would realize how many similarities exist in these tactics and methods. It certainly confirms the shadow presence of a third party working hard to impose their own playbook.

Chapter 17

The Ayers Factor

Virtually every country has individuals among their population who dream of the day when their country is ruled by some combination of socialist or communist principles. They live to promote it publicly, privately, peacefully, or in whatever fashion they can. Often, they are also willing to use violence as a way to impose their ideas.

In Uruguay, beginning in the 1970s, a collection of such individuals had been organized by a small group led by Jose Mujica and Lucia Topolansky. At the same time in America, a strikingly similar group was being assembled by A Chicago lawyer named William Ayers and his wife Bernadine Dohrn.

This struggle to use violence and coercion to achieve political goals has gone on since well before the days that Marx and Lenin. The goal is always some variation of pushing the affairs of a sovereign nation into socialist control from within. Socialism always arrives with noble-sounding goals. It never matters who ends up in charge. The result is always the same – the destruction of that nation's prosperity and the freedoms of its citizens.

The universal call of socialism always starts with appeals like this:

Workers of the world UNITE!
Throw off your oppressors!
We are equal and free under Socialism!

At least 90% of the world's population lives in countries where a very few wealthy and politically powerful elites control almost all civil rights, government jobs, and almost all of the jobs. In these countries, someone standing in the Town Square will always get a hearing:

"They have everything while you have nothing! It's not fair!"
"They are getting rich off of your hard work!"
"It's time you had some real power! We will show you how!"
"All you have to do is demand more! Let us teach you what to do!"

This is why a brief review of Uruguay's history is once again helpful. In Chapter 11, you learned the story of a committed Uruguayan anarchist and socialist named Jose

Mujica. His political saga began in the 1970s and continued for 50 years, culminating in 2010 with his election to the presidency of Uruguay. In the process he fought against both democratic governments and military dictators until finally outlasting them all to implement the socialist government of his dreams.

By Mujica's side was another anarchist and socialist, a woman named Lucia Topolansky. Topolansky was with Mujica from the beginning. Topolansky came from an educated middle-class family while Mujica's family was dirt poor. However, in many ways their stories as Tupamaros are almost mirror images of one another. Both were true believers in the cause. Both began with an early violent criminal history as they participated in crimes of all sorts to support their socialist Tupamaro movement. Some of their actions were to destabilize the government, others were to fund their movement, still others were purely acts of political terror to achieve a specific goal.

Both Mujica and Topolansky were hunted by the police and military authorities for several years for their crimes. They were both arrested several times only to later escape. After a military coup in 1973, they were captured and imprisoned, this time for over a decade. When the military junta returned power to civilian rule in 1985, the democratically elected government released them along with hundreds of others under a grant of amnesty. Along the way, the two were married and have remained so for years.

This unrepentant pair of socialists was finally able to achieve politically what they had not been able to do through violence. Mujica rose to become president of Uruguay from 2010 to 2015. Topolansky became leader of the Senate in 2009. Then, in 2017, Topolansky was appointed to the vice presidency after the Sendic financial forced him from office.

The process is more thoroughly discussed in Chapters 11 and 12. The reason it is repeated here is among the reasons I felt compelled to write this book. My goal in emigrating to America was to achieve political freedom and enjoy economic success that was no longer possible in Uruguay due to the socialist restrictions ultimately installed by people like Mujica and Topolansky.

Once in the U.S. I became an avid student of contemporary American political history. Throughout the course of my work to earn my U.S. citizenship, I realized two important truths that I still feel compelled to act on to this day. The first is that I began to see how socialism (often now called progressivism) had also rooted and was being widely adopted in America. That is why I continued to be a pro-democracy activist while I was living in Kentucky.

The second thing I discovered during this education, was that America also had its very own legendary husband-wife team of rabid socialists: William Ayers and Bernadine Dohrn. The parallel between the two of them and their Uruguayan counterparts - Mujica and Topolansky - is nothing short of amazing.

William Ayers was a key figure behind the Weather Underground that was responsible for most of the many events described in Chapter 16 - The America List. Their storied history begins about 1969 - the same time that Mujica and Topolansky were starting their socialist terrorist activities in Uruguay.

The remainder of this chapter will focus on Ayers and Dohrn. After, you will be free to draw your own conclusions about the striking similarities between both countries and both pairs of anarchists.

William Ayers, Bernadine Dohrn, Jeff Jones and Celia Sojurn were the leaders of the communist Weather Underground that they founded in the early 1970s. Their 149-page document Prairie Fire was their manifesto published in 1974. It combined everything they believed wrong in America into a single document the same way that the Tupamaros had created their own, less formal list of demands in Uruguay.

The Prairie Fire manifesto was a collection of great ways to destroy a nation but contained almost nothing about how to transform the country back into a functional and prosperous nation after almost destroying it. All of the ideas about how to rebuild were little more than an eclectic collection of cliches with almost no specifics. How appropriate that this rambling document is dedicated to Satan and over 100 other anarchists, including Che Guevara.

In the late 1960s and early 1970s America was beginning to see challenges and assaults on the ideals and institutions of American society - both the political and financial. Every country always faces problems on many fronts that need to be addressed. In the America of the 1960s, that list included the Vietnam War, segregation and racism, immigration, economic inequalities, and sexism just to name a few. Anarchists are always great at fanning the embers of discontent into infernos of anger. Then the outrage is channeled to disrupt the status quo and to help them achieve their own goals. The name Prairie Fire was adopted to show, in their words, that "a single spark can start a Prairie Fire."

Excerpts from the Prairie Fire manifesto of 1970s shown here give a sense the rhetoric and goals that the Weather Underground hoped to achieve:

> *Our final goal is the destruction of imperialism, the seizure of power, and the creation of socialism. Our strategy for this stage of the struggle is to organize the oppressed people of the imperial nation itself to join with the colonies in the attack on imperialism. This process of attacking and weakening imperialism involves the defeat of all kinds of national chauvinism and arrogance; this is a precondition to our fight for socialism.*
>
> *Socialism is the total opposite of capitalism/ imperialism. It is the rejection of empire and white supremacy. Socialism is the violent overthrow of the bourgeoisie, the establishment of the dictatorship of the proletariat, and the eradication of the social system based on profit. Socialism means control of the productive forces for the good of the whole community instead of the few who live on hilltops and in mansions. Socialism means priorities based on human need instead of corporate greed. Socialism creates the conditions for a decent and creative quality of life for all.*
>
> *May 9, 1974*
>
> *Sisters and brothers,*

> *Here is PRAIRIE FIRE, our political ideology - a strategy for anti-imperialism and revolution inside the imperial US.*
>
> *..... By constant change, that the only possibilities are victory or death.*
>
> *We have only begun. At this time, the unity and consolidation of anti-imperialist forces around a revolutionary program is an urgent and pressing strategic necessity. PRAIRIE FIRE is offered as a contribution to this unity of action and purpose. Now it is in your hands.*
>
> *Bernardine Dohrn*
> *Jeff Jones*
> *Billy Ayers*
> *Celia Sojourn*
> *For the Weather Underground*

Prior to the Weather Underground's emergence, a national student movement called Students for a Democratic Society (SDS) had organized and became active in the 1960s. It was formed to protest the U.S. government's unpopular polices and actions in the Vietnam War. Vietnam remained almost exclusively the SDS focus for their protests and civil disobedience until a splinter group emerged calling themselves the Weather Underground.

The WU proclaimed themselves to be the "action" arm of the SDS. They were actually a militant group of Marxists and communists whose goals included the violent overthrow of the United States government - far beyond simply ending the Vietnam War. They were clearly using their association with SDS as a cover for a much more militant agenda. Their crimes and attacks are detailed in The America List in Chapter 16. The vast majority of these attacks were planned and carried out by the Weathermen. This is where one begins to get a glimpse of how much more dangerous the WU would eventually become.

The information that follows comes from a wide variety of sources. Oftentimes, the same information could be found in both conservative and progressive sources, though obviously not from the same articles. For example, publications like Free Republic were generally conservative while others, like news website Truthout.org, were highly skewed in the direction of a progressive and socialist agendas. They are used as sources because the information they reported presented a fairly consistent narrative even though they come from opposite points of view. Even if there is not a clear attribution to an original source, they tell a very similar story that illustrates that Ayers and Dohrn sought the same goals as Uruguay's Mujica and Topolansky. In Uruguay, Mujica and Topolansky were eventually free to directly run for political office because of their grants of amnesty in 1985. In the United States Ayers and Dohrn instead chose a different approach.

They sought to first identify large numbers of like-minded disciples wherever they spoke or taught. Ayers' career as a tenured professor in the College of Education at the University of Chicago gave them the perfect vantage point to do this. Once identified, the pair would further their indoctrination and try to weed out the true believers in the process. Those who showed promise would be immersed into places where social injustice could be stirred into outrage.

As these disciples became more skilled, they would be inserted to participate in left-leaning causes throughout the American political landscape. In the 1970s, that left-leaning landscape was almost exclusively confined to within the Democratic Party, especially in the emerging progressive wing.

Ayers and Dohrn watched as their hand-picked leaders emerged. They would also try to guide and promote the more promising among them. By the 1980s. their efforts were beginning to yield some significant success. As they rose in prominence, they would do so with Weatherman / Marxist ideas firmly embedded in their hearts.

If this sounds far-fetched, consider how well this process worked for Ayers and Dohrn. You might recognize the names of their most influential and committed disciples:

Bill and Hillary Clinton

Barack and Michele Obama

It was at the Chicago home of Ayers and Dohrn that an up-and-coming community organizer named Barack Obama launched his political career in 1995. On that evening, a small group of very influential Democrats came to Bill Ayers' home and learned that Alice Palmer would be stepping down from the U.S Senate. The progressive-left Democrats that ran Chicago politics would need an electable candidate. It was clear that Barack Obama's political coming-out party happened right there in Bill Ayers' living room.

With Bill Ayers' and Bernardine Dohrn's backgrounds, it is hard to understand how anybody who believes in American values can enjoy a friendly relationship with them, much less for over 20 years. Ayers and Dohrn's strategy was to find individuals who sounded like supporters of America but, in private, wanted to see a solidly socialist agenda implemented in America. In other words, they believed in the exact opposite of what they proclaimed to believe publicly. They had found just such individuals when they found the Obamas.

Both Barack and Michele Obama, for example, often publicly spoke of the greatness of the American system. In private, it was clear they both initially hid a hatred of many core American values. Once you understand their very strained relationship with American traditional values, it becomes clear why they ciould privately enjoy a close friendship with people like Ayers and Dorn. It is also clear why they went to such lengths to hide it.

It is fair for the American people to ask what Barack Obama saw in Ayers, the committed anti-capitalist radical. In truth, Ayres had by this time become one of Obama's mentors. It's also fair to ask why the New York Times (and the rest of the media) was so quick to dismiss the significance of their relationship. Obama and Ayers were clearly much closer friends over decades than either of them has ever been willing to admit publicly. In fact, their repeated denials of friendship and close association have been so regular and extreme that they seem almost comical compared to the overwhelming evidence in the public record that indicates just the opposite. One of the most notable instances of this will serve as an example.

In October 2008, a John McCain campaign ad questioned why Obama maintained close ties with one of the 1960s most radical terrorist. Obama flippantly replied when questioned by the press that Ayers was just "a guy who lives in my neighborhood, not somebody who I exchange ideas with on a regular basis." What an odd response considering Obama had been essentially a high-level employee and protégé of Bill Ayers for eight years, starting in 1995.

In 1993, Ayers co-wrote and received the $50 million matching grant to create the Chicago Annenberg Challenge to restructure and influence outcomes of Chicago Public Schools. The Chicago grant was just part of the $500 million the Annenberg Foundation had pledged to 'reform' public education nationwide.

Who did Ayres pick in 1995 to be the new foundation's Chairman of the Board? Barack Obama. Obama then served in that capacity for eight years until the Challenge ended in 2003. Ayers would later brag that the Foundation had raised and spent at over $110 million to implement a "radical reform program in the Chicago Public Schools."

Ayers' use of the Challenge grant and elevation of Obama to Chairman were just two more ways for Ayers to strengthen and extend his socialist agenda. Still think Ayers was just "a guy who lives in my neighborhood, not somebody who I exchange ideas with on a regular basis?" Turns out nobody else believed him either.

It was crystal clear that Obama knew well who he was associating with. Obama also knew who was paying him to serve on not one, but two corporate boards (the Woods Fund also). At one point, the two men even shared an office! Obama surely knew what he was doing, what they were promoting, and to whom he was directing millions of donation dollars.

So, Obama continued to lie to cover up their 20-year relationship, and his long-time friend, Bill Ayers, lied right along with him. Logical and no surprise when you realize both of them are very strong believers that the ends justify the means. And say what you like, but how odd it was that Obama, a former community organizer whose only credential was a brand-new law school degree, could somehow leap to the top of a new and very prestigious foundation. Then, to the amazement of everyone (almost), he managed to follow that role by immediately getting elected to a single term in the U.S. Senate – his first public office! Obama obviously had no time for a second term because in 2007, he announced his candidacy for President of the United States. Against all odds, Obama some managed to get elected President after only that single Senate term. This was almost unprecedented in modern American politics. Yet he was also elected for a second term as well. Wow!

Obama proved himself a good orator and speaker. However, in his chest beat the heart of a racist and committed socialist. People heard him talk about wanting to "fundamentally change America" believing Obama's goal was for good. Just a quick look at today's headlines shows whet kind of transformation he was really seeking. It's no surprise that one of Obama's many nicknames was "Divider-in-Chief."

At least Jose Mujica became President of Uruguay on his own.

In his Prairie Fire manifesto, Ayers writes:

> *"We are a guerilla organization. We are communist men and women, underground in the United States for more than four years ... We need a revolutionary communist party in order to lead the struggle, give coherence and direction to the fight, seize power and build the new society ... Our intention is to disrupt the empire, to incapacitate it, to put pressure on the cracks, to make it hard to carry out its bloody functioning against the people of the world, to join the world struggle, to attack from the inside."*

Chapter 18

Toxic Connections

Barack Obama was not the only one with ties to Ayres and his supporters. In 2001, Weather Underground members were pardoned by President Bill Clinton on Clinton's last day in office. One member of the Weather Underground, Linda Sue Evans, was sentenced in 1985 to 40 years in prison for carrying a gun obtained illegally and harboring a fugitive from a robbery that resulted in two deaths. She ended up serving only 16 of the 40 years she had been sentenced because she had her sentence commuted in January 2001 by Bill Clinton.

Another former Weather Underground member, Susan Rosenberg, was caught in 1984 in possession of 740 pounds of dynamite intended for use in domestic terrorist attacks. She was sentenced to 58 years in prison. Rosenberg was also allegedly involved in the 1981 Brink's armored car robbery. President Bill Clinton also commuted Rosenberg's sentence in 2001, freeing her after only 16 years of a 58-year sentence in an action widely covered at the time as a pardon

Hillary Clinton also had connections with both Dohrn and terrorists from South America. Otherwise, for example, why would a Senator from New York visit Uruguay to attend a ceremony to witness the transfer of power to newly-elected President Jose Mujica, the Tupamaro terrorist? Perhaps it was to also draw attention to Mujica's support for the same type of socialist health care reforms that Hillary Clinton was pushing in America

During her visit, Mrs. Clinton praised the strength of Uruguay's political system, now hopelessly socialist. She was quoted saying:

> *"I wish to not only congratulate the President-Elect Mujica and his new government, but to applaud the way in which the government is unifying and bringing together even opposition parties. Indeed, Uruguayans are rightly proud of their leaders and their democracy."*

Another interesting name who gets involved with the Ayers and Dohrn's time line is Massachusetts Senator John Kerry. Ayers and Dohrn led several Free Gaza Movement initiatives, including attempted marches into the Gaza Strip. In March, 2010, Kerry wrote a letter in support of a "humanitarian delegation from Massachusetts" to Gaza that included Ayers and Dohrn. They later published on their blog about how they used Kerry's letter at the U.S. Embassy in Cairo while attempting to pressure Egypt to let their group into Gaza. Images of the letter were also posted online on their website.

How can a person who attacks others by calling them a radical extremist continue to employ radical extremists as the Clinton's have done?

In South America, Jose Mujica was finally elected President of Uruguay in 2010. Remember that Mujica had bombed American companies and American banks in Uruguay. He was also involved directly in the murder of American citizen and FBI agent, Dan Mitrione. Imagine the irony when the Uruguayan version of the William Ayers finally gets to meet Ayer's most wildly successful disciple – Barack Obama.

American President Barack Obama and Uruguayan President Jose Mujica met in 2012 in Cartagena, Colombia. They had dinner together and spoke for over an hour. After dinner, Obama stated that he was delighted with his meeting with the domestic terrorist who also happened to be the current President of Uruguay. Mujica remarked he was impressed with the fine thinking of President Obama. And how equally odd that the socialist superstars of Uruguay and the United States would one day meet and declare support for each other. I wonder if anyone took note that Jose Mujica, Uruguay's counterpart to William Ayers finally gets to meet Ayers's most wildly successful disciple – Barack Obama.

Sometimes things are not always as they seem and we need wisdom to tell the difference. So, in the same way my father once asked me who was the real bad influence, I now ask, "Who are really the socialists here?"

If you are still with me at this stage, you have by now come to realize that I don't believe any of these amazing events and relationships are just coincidences either. The forces that are behind this agenda are devious, extensive, well-funded, and organized.

Chapter 19

Moving Forward

An iconic face from my past reappeared on my TV not long ago. I was watching a big protest march in Los Angeles. On the screen were hundreds of people waving flags and signs while marching enthusiastically. There are so many protests in Los Angeles these days, I'm surprised there isn't a dedicated cable channel for them.

Why did this one catch my attention? What made it special? It was then I realized there were so many marchers proudly wearing t-shirts with that identical face on them. It was the same face I had seen on walls, flags, posters, and propaganda in South America. It was the same face that, for decades, had been used and abused by radical left groups as a symbol of the Marxist revolution. It was the face of Che Guevara.

I had grown up with that face plastered everywhere. It was fairly common – even expected in a land where socialism had taken such powerful roots. Seeing people honor this man and seeing his face so prominently displayed here in America was a shock I was not expecting.

That TV event from LA was now archived somewhere in the back of my brain where it stayed until I started my research into the Ayers - Obama relationship. I had just gotten a copy of Ayers' manifesto, <u>Prairie Fire</u>. There, in the dedication, was that same image of the El Che that I had been seeing my entire life.

Bill Ayers and his wife, Bernadine Dohrn had traveled to Cuba in the 1960s to see the Cuban revolution close up. Undoubtedly, they also received some training, perhaps even training on how to handle the explosives they would later be fond of using. Ayers and Dohrn had become well-known leaders of the American Marxist movement by this time. Meetings with high-level Cuban revolutionaries such as Che or even Castro himself are easy to envision. The founder and leader of the fledgling Uruguayan Tupamaro movement, Raul Sendic, had also visited Cuba in the 1960s for the same reasons.

In 2004, one of the first decisions of the new socialist Uruguayan government was to resume diplomatic relations with Cuba. The relationship had been broken by the previous government due to well-documented and extensive violations of human rights in Cuba. This is the same Cuba in which Ernesto Che Guevara helped to establish the communist government so people could become "fair and free".

In 2014, America was shocked when President Barack announced his plan to re-establish diplomatic relations with Cuba. He also removed Cuba from the State Department's list of nations known to sponsor terrorism even though Cuba was still doing so.

The announcement from Uruguay in 2004 was expected. The U.S. announcement in 2014 was a shock to me as well. It was like a bad dream in which you are running to escape and you finally reach a place to hide. You close the door only to open your eyes to find the evil you were escaping is sitting right there in the room waiting for you.

My eyes were certainly opening to America. I was here living, learning, working, and healing. I was also now asking myself about many things. The answers to those questions suggested that those opposed to American values of democracy and capitalism were much farther along than I had realized in their quest to destroy them. The circle now seemed unbroken somehow. It connected from the

Tupamaros to Che Guevara to socialist Jose Mujica in Uruguay to Bill Ayers to Barack Obama to the cancer of socialism in America then back again.

I had left Uruguay for America because it looked like politically, Uruguay would be lost for generations to come. Now I was a naturalized American citizen with invested here. Yet now I could clearly see the same threats aggressively chipping away at America and showing few signs of stopping.

That was when I realized it was time to stop looking for something better. It was time to be a part of building something better. I could not allow 250 years of the greatest democratic republic in history be destroyed. I now knew why I was here. I also knew what I must do. The future for my family and my adopted homeland depends on it.

* * * *

For the first time, I understood what must have been going through the mind of the man in the gray suit as he sat alone with his newborn son in 1971. I felt the hopes and fears he must have felt on that winter's night in the hospital where he and I spent our first day together. For him then, and for me now, there is nowhere else to go.

It is time to fight.

Chapter 20

The Border Crisis

By this time, I was now living in Arizona. I had also started a successful business and my life was definitely improving. I began considering how to best help reverse the slide into socialism that seemed to be all around me. Our home at the time was in a suburban community south of Phoenix, Arizona. To the south and west, there were a number of farms, several factories, and a whole lot of open desert. One hundred miles away was the U.S. border with Mexico.

Along the 1933-mile length of that border, a crisis has exploded that is getting worse every day. Existing U.S. laws are being broken regularly or ignored or deliberately not enforced. President Barack Obama took office in 2008 with his promise to fundamentally change America. Few could imagine how that transformation would turn the U.S −

Mexico border into a no-man's land where drug smuggling, human trafficking, and practically zero enforcement of border access laws would be the order of the day

There is a clear plan at work here that daily makes a mockery of U.S. sovereignty. It makes it look like the most powerful country in the world can't even control its own borders. The shift toward what many now call Open Borders, started with President Bill Clinton in 1992. Open Borders has been actively supported by the people who have held the highest positions in the government for 19 of the last 31 years. Clinton allowed a very lax policy of border enforcement to remain in place while at the same time stating how critical it was for the border to be lawful and secure. That was clearly not true. What was true that such a lax enforcement policy was nothing more than an attempt to help the Democratic party swell its ranks with new supporters. Why wouldn't they? New immigrants, legal or otherwise, are seen to be strongly socialist in their leanings and thus much more likely to vote for the Democrat's strong socialist agenda. That is why the Democratic strategy for decades has been to relentlessly push for citizenship amnesty that would grant voting rights to those millions of illegal border crossers already here.

The reality is that the Democratic progressives have no intention of restricting unlawful border crossing. With

President Joe Biden in office, they are not just turning a blind eye. They are now actively working to dismantle the security of those borders. The truth is that a southern border with little or no restrictions is actually a GOAL of those socialist haters of American capitalism and democracy. Here is one ironic recent examples of Democratic border enforcement double-speak.

Former Tucson police chief Chris Magnus is testifying, hoping to be confirmed to head the nation's border enforcement authority - Customs and Border Protection. A Senator at his hearing told Magnus he was "walking into a chaotic situation where we have the highest number of illegal crossings in the history of our country. What is your plan?"

Magnus responded,
"I don't disagree with you that the numbers are very high. But the bottom line still remains that, first and foremost, we need to enforce the law."

Say what you like, the Biden administration has demonstrated repeatedly that they have no intention of enforcing the law along the border. And as a bonus. if you are a part of the majority socialist Democratic apparatus, once again one can see that it apparently doesn't matter whether you tell the truth in a confirmation hearing just like it doesn't matter whether you uphold the Constitution on your watch. No one holds you accountable.

What follows in this chapter highlights the current and inexcusable state of crime and lawlessness that exists long the U.S. – Mexico border.

Illegal Immigration

Everyone understands why people who are impoverished or who live in constant fear of gang violence or government corruption are willing to make great sacrifices to come to America. Millions of people for decades have been willing to violate U.S. law just to have a chance to be here. But to understand is not to justify. It was difficult for me to comprehend why the United States immigration system did not have protections built in for American citizens to control the tidal wave of people coming across the Mexico border.

First, I thought flow of people across America's southern border was simply about the U.S. desire for cheap labor. But this is only a small part of the answer.

In reality, cheap labor in the U.S. is an effect of immigration, not the cause of it. There are many reasons people are willing to cross the border illegally into this country. It has always been a dangerous and sometimes deadly trip. Today, it is far more difficult than ever because the cartel syndicates now control almost every means of access to the Mexican side of the border prior to cross into the U.S.

Still, the main thing that compels millions of people from Mexico and far beyond to make journey is hope. That hope comes in many different forms. People want to come and be able to live free. They want to feed their families. They want to escape the gangs, the violence, and government corruption that surrounds them at home.

The reports from relatives in already in the U.S. plus the endless rumors they hear creates a powerful image of an America where they can literally walk right across the border with minimal resistance and have a life. Once safely across, they will get free food stamps, housing, free medical care, a cell phone, and welfare – all just for being here. As if this was not enough, then they hear of the many private charity programs that provide clothing, dental services, furniture, household goods, even money to help paying bills. Now, there is even a widespread movement in largely Democratic states to provide people in the U.S. illegally with driver's licenses, and unemployment benefits. In the extreme, places like Vermont and New York City are registering non-citizen illegal immigrants to vote!

Unchecked border migration is at an all-time high in almost virtually every category. The toll of human suffering is enormous. People regularly die of starvation, exposure, and sickness. Literally every single border crosser is victimized in some way by the cartel syndicates that now control every aspect of their trip across the border. Women and girls are abused regularly with sexual abuse being the most horribly common experience.

The Texas Public Policy Group reports regularly on the current border crisis. Their in-depth research has concluded that President Biden has made it abundantly clear that his administration does not wish to stop illegal immigration, nor does it wish to enable necessary enforcement of the immigration laws that are on the books.

It remains astounding to me that these kinds of deliberate actions are a daily occurrence on the part of Federal officials, all the way up to President Biden himself. These are the people who have SWORN A CONSTITUTIONAL OATH TO PREVENT THIS VERY THING.

Consider the irony that in the last 30 days, President Biden has announced his plan to forgive up to $1 trillion dollars in student loan debt in a horribly inequitable fashion. He has also announced the hiring of 87,000 more armed IRS agents who will be targeting taxpaying Americans to get more money from them. How much extra money did he propose for law enforcement and humanitarian aid at the border? Zero!

What is happening to our sovereign American Republic? People with little or no future are willing to break U.S. law and make the journey. What they don't realize is what they will find once they do reach this border that they are so anxious to cross. They should instead be prepared to encounter horrors and abuse so extreme that it will crush the hope that brought them there in the first place. Even still, the realities of the abuse and violence they will experience at the hands of the cartels have not deterred record numbers of people from coming.

Here are some of the everyday experiences they will experience along their journey and once they arrive at the border.

Cartel Activity

One of the most terrible affronts to the American people is the way both the Obama and Biden administrations have turned a blind eye to the operation of the Mexican drug cartels along the border. The U.S. offers only token resistance along the border while doing almost nothing to enlist Mexican authorities in the fight. This has left the cartels free to organize and take control of all illegal border activity in ways that are horrible in the extreme. The FBI reports now that one of their biggest concerns now is the explosion of violence that is being seen to keep their empires of drug smuggling and human trafficking operating smoothly. It's not just the thousands of murders, it's the ways people are being raped, killed, and mutilated in the must dehumanizing ways. Running afoul of the cartels frequently means first having a loved one killed or violated to send a message, then they come for you.

Human Trafficking

Slavery is alive and well today in the form of human trafficking along the entirety of the border. Under the Biden administration, however, human traffickers are now busier than ever. Trafficking has become a growth industry and there are now more recognized forms of trafficking than ever. Most notably, trafficking includes forced sexual exploitation, especially among women and children of both genders. It also includes domestic servitude and slave labor for mostly factory and agricultural work.

Even after their arrival in the U.S., they are still held captives in some form against their will and coerced into a role they do not want. Victims of human trafficking experience extreme physical and psychological abuse while being isolated from the world. That abuse is just one of many tools their captors use to control them.

Adam Isaacson is a reporter for a widely-respected human rights journal published by WOLA.org. In a recent article from April 2022, he makes a number of observations while reporting from Texas that perfectly summarize today's reality along the entire length of the U.S. border.

"It was my fourth day of my visit to the border region...Part of me was beginning to wonder whether the United States' border and migration policies were somehow being designed with input from the Mexican organized crime groups that prey on migrants. It would be hard to devise a system that benefits these cartels more than the current one does... Mexican organized crime has locked down the routes across the border...Those who can pay several-thousand-dollar fees cross with cartel-sanctioned smugglers. It's a huge moneymaker for organized crime, and for the corrupt Mexican security and migration officials who get paid to look the other way.

I was struck by the level of control that organized crime has over the lives of residents, and especially of migrants."

It was not long ago that guiding small groups of immigrants across the border for a fee used to be the domain of independent smugglers. Now, through extreme violence and corruption of Mexican officials, virtually all of the cross-border groups have come under cartel control and are led by armed and cartel-sanctioned "coyotes" or guides.

Sex Trafficking

Sex trafficking deserves special mention here because it is one of the most degrading and abusive forms of human trafficking. Mexico has for years been a global center of the sex trafficking trade and it is especially prevalent along the border with Arizona. A trafficked young teen girl has long been one of the most valuable commodities in the human slave trade. She may be sold for tens of thousands of dollars or turned out as a prostitute where her exploitation can ultimately earn hundreds of thousands of dollars for her captor. In one recent case, a number of young Hispanic girls were found as captives in apartments in Queens against their will. They were driven from appointment to appointment to have sex with men. An assistant special agent for Homeland Security spoke off the record about it. "They see 15, 20 men in an evening and all money is handed over to the trafficker."

The Coalition Against Trafficking In Women estimates that 60% of Latin American women and children who set out to cross the border alone or with smugglers have been caught by the cartels and abused.

Child Trafficking

Perhaps even more horrifying than sex trafficking is the trafficking of children. Sexual exploitation of children as prostitutes or forcing then into the production of pornography still ranks among the top reasons children are taken in this way.

A new type of child trafficking "market" has also just emerged because the Biden administration is now giving priority to process immigrant family units with minors within 72 hours. In response, the cartels have started 'renting" many of the thousands of unaccompanied children available to single male crossers so they can be processed faster using the "family" designation and be on their way sooner. They are given paper citations to appear in court as much as 8 months in the future and are then released in the U.S. where they simply disappear. The child is then smuggled back into Mexico only to repeat the process again.

To make matters even worse, child trafficking is now going both ways across the border. Abduction or coercion of runaways and outright kidnapping of children in the U.S. for transport and sale to buyers in Mexico and beyond is also on the rise. An attractive American minor child can literally be worth their weight in gold to these networks.

How a civilized country like the U.S. can accept the inaction, even the complicity of multiple Democratic administrations to barely lift a finger to stop this is beyond my ability to comprehend. But I am committing myself to do what I can to stop it and you should too. How do we ever plan to give account of ourselves one day and say that we knew about this and did nothing?

Drug Smuggling

The best way to summarize what is happening to drug enforcement efforts along the border is to begin by saying there are almost no remaining cross-border efforts at enforcement. It is now up to the U.S. alone to catch what they can. The DEA has indicated that the cartels have become so powerful they have corrupted the government in Mexico almost completely. As a result, Mexican officials have all but ceased the cross-border cooperation that is essential for any meaningful enforcement to take place. Cocaine and methamphetamine continues to be popular exports to the U.S. but Fentanyl has quickly become the cartel's preferred drug of choice. It is cheap, easily produced, and widely available from their new partners, the Chinese. Note the CDC has just reported that the number one cause of death among 18-45 year-olds in the U.S. is now drug overdose and 70% of those are from fentanyl.

It is known that most of the drugs smuggled into the country come in through ports of entry. However, the cartels are constantly developing new ways to bring drugs across the border. Even the traditional method of forcing border crossers to carry backpacks full of drugs has also become more sophisticated. Now crossers are being made to wear camouflage clothing as well to further avoid detection, then given a camo backpack full of drugs as well to drop inside the U.S. border.

Media Complicity

Over the past few decades, the national media outlets have become the silent supporter of the border crisis and the illegal immigrant invasion. When a crime is committed by an someone illegally in this country, for example, the media will simply bury it or be too busy to even report it.

This mainstream media bias has by now been well-documented by every journalistic source that isn't them! The way they block out or completely fail to report stories of crimes committed by illegal immigrants has everything to do with their complicity with the larger Democratic party in general. They constantly maneuver to put Democrat or socialist causes and people in the best possible light. They also tend to instantly grab and run with every tidbit and news story then can find that presents conservatives and Republicans in a bad light.

Time and again the national media networks have been caught running a negative news story that simply isn't true or reporting before verifying even the most basic facts only to have to issue a retraction later. Many times, they have been caught in reporting that proved to be outright lies. This includes fabricated quotes or video footage that they have doctored to promote a false narrative.

Unethical reporting or ignoring important stories about illegal immigrants or immigration policy is clearly only a part of a much larger belief held by the major media outlets that everything conservative or Republican should either be attacked or ignored depending on which suits their narrative best.

Is Amnesty the Solution?

Massive amnesty will not achieve justice or "normalization" either. Instead, the intention of amnesty is to alter the electorate. My question is how can we preserve our America when the other side seems to be on steroids trying to destroy it? I want every politician running for office how they will defend our Constitutional rights if they succeed in just handing the vote to over thirty million more Democratic socialists.

It wasn't clear to me when I first arrived in 2003 why so many groups claiming to have a humanitarian agenda were so anxious for wide open borders. Not long after being elected, then-president Barack Obama threatened Congress that he would not consider any immigration reform if it did not include a path to citizenship to the tens of millions of people already in the U.S. illegally. Why would he do that when it was it was clear that so many of them had absolutely no love or respect for this nation?

I finally realized what supporters of socialism in the U.S. at every level already knew. Mass amnesty would immediately help the Democratic party swell its ranks with over 20-30 million new members. This would quickly hasten their goal to replace American capitalism and democracy with communist socialism that would define it for decades to come.

We can believe in fairness, freedom, diversity and secure borders, but no one should be given a pass for breaking our laws and sneaking into our country. We have a right to not only expect that, but to demand it. Those who say otherwise have an agenda, pure and simple, and it certainly isn't found in the Declaration of Independence, the Constitution, or the Bill of Rights.

Don't think so? Consider what has happened in California - a state where former President Ronald Reagan once served two terms as governor. Reagan had an amnesty bill passed in 1987 that granted citizenship to almost 3 million previously illegal immigrants. A large percentage of those immigrants were living in California at that time and they were overwhelmingly Hispanic. Hispanics are now the majority there and along with out-of-control socialism, their presence has transformed the Golden State into a permanent socialist state.

Look at California today. They have become one of the most heavily taxed and regulated states in the country with one of the least business-friendly environments. Their socialist policies have transformed California into a haven for homelessness and crime that actually saw the state's population drop in both 2020 and 2021 for the first time in more than a century. Yet California voters keep returning Democratic representatives to office who continue to accelerate California's decline into a lawless socialist utopia. Sounds like the definition of insanity at work. It is an eventual setup for the painful reality how socialism continues to function until it finally runs out of other people's money.

California is also clearly a model for what will happen to the rest of the country if amnesty legislation is passed. Do you see your liberties flourishing under their socialism or becoming more and more endangered? The socialist track record virtually guarantees an unfavorable outcome.

Chapter 21

Thomas's Flag

It was Memorial Day in 2014 as I sat in my living room. The TV was playing off to the side and the afternoon had grown increasingly hot and humid. The events of the past few months were still fresh on my mind. I had finally put behind me an ongoing fight from the last couple of years that had left me battered. I arrived in America in 2003 with a love of democracy deep within my soul.

One of my first goals was to understand more about the American political landscape. I was able to quickly see that the values of the so-called Democratic Party were almost completely in line with the socialist ideals of the Broad Front I had left behind in Uruguay. Instead, I saw that Republican

Party represented most of the democratic ideals my father taught me. I watched local politics as much as I could while I worked hard at raising and supporting my family.

Over time I became known to people within the Republican party throughout Kentucky. Many people found my love for American democracy and the story of my life as a Latino immigrant the very symbol of what this country stood for. I had legally come to the U.S., established a successful career, and was now taking the steps to become a United States citizen. I also was encouraged to write about my experiences to inspire others. I published those stories in a book in 2013.

I began getting invitations to speak and I became a voice of encouragement, especially to other Latinos that they were welcome in the Republican party. There were even whispers of my future as a candidate once I became a naturalized U.S. citizen. However, the more I saw, the more I realized that there was not one, but two sets of priorities within the Republican Party. The first priority was the one they advertised – get Republican candidates with strong values elected to continue building a strong American democracy.

The second priority was a very important set of unspoken rules. The goal of that version of the party was to perpetuate the party first. Getting the candidates elected came after. As a result, the kind of candidate the Republican party supports and promotes looks different. The favored candidate becomes someone who will go along to get along first. Words tend to be endless and accomplish little. People deserve representatives who will fight for the things that will help them, not just talk about them. I am a fighter for the cause of democracy. It is deeds that matter.

That kind of endless talking without action was one of the main reasons for the failure of the Colorado party, and ultimately democracy, in my native Uruguay. It led to too much fighting within the party which often brought the process of governing to a halt. Lack of progress from those repeated stalemates gave Broad Front the perfect chance to oust them because the Colorado party got so little done to help the country.

The events of the past few months were still fresh on my mind, the ongoing fight over political priorities had left me battered. I was disappointed by the apathy, but not defeated.

I had placed my American flag to be seen through my living room window. I looked at it and decided it was not enough so I sat down at my computer to search for the another one. Somehow, I would find the perfect companion for this flag.

I scrolled endlessly through many online auction sites. The list of available flags seemed repetitive and never-ending. Suddenly, one really caught my attention. At the top listing on one of the search pages, I found a listing for an actual World War II Veteran's Burial flag. One magical click and I was reading the item's description. The description said the seller had purchased it at an estate auction. The flag was still in its special wooden box and had not been claimed by anyone in the Veteran's family.

The television playing in the background drew my attention away from the computer screen to a video of the D-Day invasion. The timing could have not been an accident. I watched soldiers bravely swarming out of landing craft and storming the beaches. Bombs were exploding and gun fire was everywhere. I watched for a few more minutes before returning my attention back to the flag on the auction listing before me.

Now I had a thousand questions. To whom did this abandoned flag belong? Who would abandon such a flag? Who was this warrior who had been able to survive WWII, and return home to live another fifty years?

The veteran's first name was Thomas. I will not disclose his last name out of respect for the privacy of his family. Thomas had earned the honor of having the American flag, this flag, draped over his casket to honor his military service.

Here was the flag he fought to defend that represented the values of his nation. His flag – now abandoned and for sale to complete strangers on the internet.

A soldier is willing to fight and ultimately die to preserve for themselves and others the legacy of freedom and liberty. Nothing matters more than the transfer to these values to the next generation. This flag is a solemn and symbolic way of passing along those principles and values of our nation. I was quiet suddenly, even while sitting there in my living room with bombs exploding on the television. I was overwhelmed by the tragedy of this abandoned flag.

In an instant I realized why I was touched so deeply by this particular flag. This abandoned flag represented perfectly what was happening to America as a nation. A whole generation seems to be walking away, abandoning the principles and values symbolized in this flag for hundreds of years. Have we so easily forgotten the sacrifices which have been made on our behalf so we can stand free in this place, at this time? I had watched the same thing happen in my beloved Uruguay and I am now watching the same thing happen in my adopted home of America.

I decided to watch the fate of the flag online to see if anyone would come to its rescue. Over the next five days I checked regularly on the progress of the auction. The auction was scheduled to end on Saturday and it expired before I could bid. The auction was over. No bids!

I messaged the seller and made an offer. I had little hope of acquiring it but to my surprise, my offer was accepted! We closed the deal and the flag, no longer abandoned, arrived on June 4, 2014 - just two days before the 70th Anniversary of D-Day.

I placed the shipping box on the coffee table and sat down just looking at it, unable to open it and unsure what to do. I gathered my racing thoughts and I called to my daughter to join me. I told her the story and spoke to her about the flag. I told her what I knew about the man behind the flag. I marveled at how it had arrived two days before D-Day 70th Anniversary.

I eventually opened the box while still speaking to my daughter about the flag and what it represented. I asked her to never abandon this flag. After all we had been through, it now seemed to be part of our obligation as new citizens and assimilated immigrants to work alongside natural Americans to keep these values alive. Our family shares the same principles and values with those who fought and those still fighting to make this nation everything it aspires to become. The America we came to join is prosperous, a society where children can grow up free, receive a good education, live productive lives and enjoy the peace provided by those who fought before us to keep that dream alive.

    I rescued Thomas's flag, but it was clear that was not all that was required of me. The intense emotion that this flag brought to my life was now compelling me to do more. I needed to share the dream that is America. I needed to share what I see in our future through my personal experience. I needed to teach what history is revealing to us and what we must do to make things even better.

    Thomas's flag now rests safely in my home in a place of honor. Yet today, the principles and values it represents are at grave risk. They cannot be preserved for future generations by letting someone else do the hard work. We need to bring the fight to all of America's enemies – foreign and domestic. Thomas fought against totalitarian forces to preserve our freedom and liberty in his day. He did his part. Now it's up to us to take up the same mantle and do ours.

    Today I'm writing to challenge the reader, asking to revive and build upon the effort Thomas made, so his fight will not have been in vain. We have an obligation to our children just as Thomas had to the children of his generation. Future generations need the symbol of the flag to rally around in times of trouble and confusion. More importantly, they need to understand and support the principles which preserve a free society. The significance of the issues, the times we are living in and what appears to be coming in our future are alarming signs. We need to pay attention, there is no other option than to shake off the apathy and get moving.

Hard work, sacrifice, and innovation are important ingredients of the past two and a half centuries that have brought success and prosperity in America. Affluence and complacency have combined to drive the important principles from our collective memory, leaving us in peril. But the worst enemy we confront today is apathy,

Aristotle said,

"Tolerance and apathy are the last virtues of a dying society,"

The only way to defeat the crisis ahead is through vigilance and action,

Thomas Jefferson also said it well,

"Eternal vigilance is the price of liberty'. "When governments fear the people there is liberty. When the people fear the government there is tyranny."

Thomas's flag has been restored to a place of honor. It's stars are symbol of the heavens, the red represents the blood spilled to protect the nation, the blue stands for honor, perseverance and vigilance, and the white for liberty and justice.

It is our flag, the symbol of our history and values.

It is Thomas's flag, the symbol of one man's sacrifice.

Now it is up to each of us to not allow it to fade.

Chapter 21

Rising to the Challenge

"Every empire eventually falls."

I have heard this phrase many times. Instead of presuming this to be true, these are the real questions me must answer:

- How do we prevent America's demise?
- What must we do to stop this failure?

What we call the miracle of America - the American spirit - cannot stay alive if we constantly undermine it with communist or socialist principles. It will fall without the vigilance and effort of its citizens.

I strongly believe the time is now to take action. We can bring America back from the edge but it won't happen if we stay on the couch or sit in front of a computer. It will first take reflection, wisdom, and most importantly - courage.

The question is: Are you ready to take action? If you are not, you must be prepared to fall.

We are living in difficult times and the absence of trust in the press and the government is unprecedented. But remember, if you give up and stop caring what is happening around you, you have already given away too much. Politics has become a dirty word. Realize, however, that it is politics that shapes and interacts with everything around you. Jobs, taxes, freedom, education, civil liberties, security, and personal happiness - they are all directly affected.

America was birthed as a Republic requiring the always vigilant eye of its people. We must also recognize the attempts to inject socialist ideals and principles because they will take us away from the correct path. These radical changes depart from the core of our democratic ideals. These radical changes are voiced by those who for decades have vowed to destroy the America we love.

Our current situation is not entirely the fault of those who oppose the founding principles that has made America the great nation that it is. Much of the blame rests with the leaders we have chosen. By that I mean the leaders who have failed to represent democratic values and the people who love them. It takes courage to resist those who would tear down the Constitution and founding ideals. In past decades, that courage has been in very short supply. Our only hope as a nation depends on our determination to think long term and take bold courageous action because we have reached the crisis level.

The political class has become cowardly and too focused on their own self-interest instead of representing the democratic ideals we need. Too many of us are suffering from apathy - believing that what we think or say or do makes little difference. This combined cowardice and apathy is a recipe for disaster.

But remember, we can change this. We can turn this around. But it is not possible to do so unless we all pitch in. It is not a simple matter of just changing the politicians in our state houses or in Washington DC. It requires that we replace them with people who have not lost sight of the importance of the Constitution or of the democratic ideals and rule of law it represents. That means finding people who don't give in to special interests for the sake of convenience or personal gain. The search is not going to be easy.

I have lived an intense life. I have confronted many issues. I have succeeded in overcoming some of them and I have failed in others. In failure, I have started over. Winston Churchill once said, *"success consists of going from failure to failure without loss of enthusiasm."*

The reason I am writing this book is not because my story is important. It is because I have an exceptional love for the country of my origin, and my adopted country, America. I have affirmed my belief that democracy is the only system that can deliver on the freedoms promised in the Constitution. I am also equally convinced that we cannot keep these freedoms alive if we don't again become vigilant or active in defending them.

I have seen first-hand what you probably have not - the death of democracy at the hands of socialism. For this reason, I am compelled to share with you those experiences that shaped my life in the hopes that they will not similarly shape yours. I do not want my life to be seen as a story of struggle but a story of overcoming struggle to achieve success. By now I hope you understand the significant role that the miracle of America has played in giving me hope and a future.

America is not a solution; it is an environment. It is also an ideal that a people can work together to create solutions to our problems. It is a laboratory where you can create your own formula and develop your own dreams.

My life is filled with memories of how I struggled to achieve my goals. If the solutions to our problems are given as handouts, they have no virtue. When I decided to run my first marathon, the experience was extreme. There I was in the middle of nowhere with my thoughts questioning me over and over. My body told me to quit and my thoughts kept telling me that I was not good enough to complete a marathon. But I was determined.

I kept running and running until I finally crossed that finish line and received my first recognition medal for having completed such a difficult task. Recently I had an opportunity to look at that medal again. The memories flooded back about what I went through and the satisfaction I felt having received it as a symbol of that achievement.

This is what it feels like to achieve a tough goal. Throwing off the influences of socialism that infect America at every level will be far harder than running any marathon but infinitely more rewarding.

What can I do?

There is a ground swell of change to take back America that is rising and must continue. Start by looking at the published platforms of both the Republican and Democratic Parties. Which of them best reflects your values and the America you want? No matter what your background, race, gender, religion, make sure your voice is heard. Meantime, stop putting this off. It IS up to us.

Here are 27 things you can do right now. Today.

1. Read this book and give a copy to 2 other people.
2. Begin to speak up about things that matter.
3. Vote for the right candidates and issues every time the voting booth is open.
4. Educate yourself about the candidates and the issues.
5. Remove politicians from office who are unraveling America.
6. Get involved in politics in your area.
7. Volunteer to pass out literature or make phone calls.
8. Go to school board and city council meetings.
9. Volunteer for organizations working to create the America you value.
10. Ask questions at candidate forums.
11. Fly an American Flag.
12. Read and pass out copies of the Declaration of Independence and the Constitution.
13. Pass petitions to get the right people and issues on the ballot.
14. Run for office yourself.
15. Change one thing in your life for the better.
16. Commit yourself to the America you want your kids to inherit.
17. Keep America – its people and institutions - held up in prayer.

18. Work at a polling place on election day. You even get paid.
19. Stop leaving the outcomes up to someone else.
20. Find a reliable source for news you can trust.
21. Laugh more.
22. Find like-minded friends you can discuss things with.
23. Become a precinct committeeman for your district.
24. Help get friends, co-workers, neighbors, and family members registered to vote.
25. Watch fewer puppy videos on the internet and start learning about the issues.
26. Drive people to vote on election day.
27. Watch debates between candidates on TV.

American citizenship is very much these things and more. I chose to become a citizen of the United States because I love and respect what America stands for. If I hadn't gone through that process and the struggle, I do not think I would have as much appreciation for how meaningful it is. It's always been the case that something achieved means far more than something that we are just given.

As you have read in these chapters, the obstacles in my life have been many and difficult. Giving in to apathy and self-pity were never options for me and they should not be for you either. We have difficult times ahead that we must handle together as a society. We need wisdom to find the real leaders among us for there are far too many deceivers who want to be in charge. This is what we must be alert and vigilant against.

A long time ago I realized that personal and collective challenges to the future of America are already here. I understand also that if the American people do not choose to be involved, it will be impossible to keep our values and principles alive. Those values have been constantly hammered and under attack for a long time. I see how the nation where I was born has languished in history and I do not plan to live through it again here in my new home.

Thomas Jefferson was not born on American soil because the Virginia of his birth was still part of Great Britian! What Jefferson had was an undeniable love of freedom from tyranny that resulted in the founding of this nation. That process had cost him and all of the signers of the Declaration of Independence most everything they owned. Some even paid with their lives. The cause was so important that they mutually pledged "to each other our Lives, our Fortunes and our sacred Honor."

Most importantly, Jefferson understood what was at stake and what would be required to preserve it. He understood that

> *"the democracy will cease to exist when you take away from those who are willing to work and give it to those who would not."*

Epilogue

In 2003, in a courtroom in Lexington, Kentucky I became a U.S. citizen. Once the judge had concluded his remarks, we exited through the same doors that we had entered, this time as Americans. We left the building on that brisk morning in October. Where the sun was strong and the skies were extremely blue. The setting was almost perfect. I stood on the stairs of the courthouse contemplating the skies, my future, and what had just occurred.

I thought of James Madison's words:

"Every man who loves his country, every man who loves liberty, ought to have it ever before his eyes, that he may cherish in his heart, a due attachment to the union of America and be able to set a due value on the means of preserving it."

Before I resumed my walk, I looked down at the Citizenship Certificate I now clutched in my hands. After 26 years, I had my name back. America had returned my identity. The plans to make me into somebody else had failed completely. The pain and the hatred were gone as it had never existed.

I walked across the square with my family and my new fellow Americans. I felt as though I was reborn that day through America and into liberty and freedom. But I was also reborn into the power of obligations that I had contracted along with my new home. I owe this nation everything, especially the miracle of my rebirth.

GOD BLESS AMERICA